Why Our High Schools Need the Arts

Jessica Hoffmann Davis

Teachers College, Columbia University
New York and London

National Art Education Association
Reston, Virginia

Published simultaneously by Teachers College Press, 1234 Amsterdam Avenue, New York, NY 10027 and The National Art Education Association, 1806 Robert Fulton Drive, Suite 300, Reston, VA 20191

Library of Congress Cataloging-in-Publication Data

Davis, Jessica Hoffmann.
Why our high schools need the arts / Jessica Hoffmann Davis.
    p. cm.
  Includes bibliographical references and index.
  ISBN 978-0-8077-5286-9 (pbk. : alk. paper)
  1. Arts—Study and teaching (Secondary)—United States.
  2. Education, Secondary—Aims and objectives—United States.
  I. Title.
  NX303.D38 2012   700.71'273—dc23

ISBN 978-0-8077-5286-9 (paper)

Printed on acid-free paper
Manufactured in the United States of America

19   18   17   16   15   14   13   12   8   7   6   5   4   3   2   1

For my Grandchildren
Stay in School and Make Art

CONTENTS

ACKNOWLEDGMENTS

For their vision and support, I am grateful to my editor, Carole Saltz, and to Emily Renwick, Karl Nyberg, and Jennifer Baker-Henry at Teachers College Press. Endless thanks go to the many high school students and teachers who contributed to this work by speaking with me directly or completing written surveys. Their real names are not mentioned within, but their rich experiences and powerful voices resound throughout this text. I thank the alumni and current students of the Arts in Education Program at the Harvard Graduate School of Education who participated themselves or helped me connect with others. Bless you. I am indebted to authentic ally Richard Olsen for sharing his beautiful new memoir and to Monique Devine and Ian Torney for inadvertently kick-starting this work. I am filled with appreciation and applause for: Anne Armstrong, Rikki Asher, Erica Randall Beam, C. William Bennett, Rhoda Bernard, Julie Bernson, Jack Bryan, M. J. Benson, Ivana Chubbuck, Dani Coleman, Benjamin Davis, E.J.K.F. Davis, Nicholas Davis, Brian Devine, Toby Dewey, Lynn Ditchfield, Bradley Diuguid, Tracie Dunn, Gary Jim Daichandt, John Flynn, Janet Muse Gray, Kristen Greer-Paglia, Irving Hamer, Lloyd Hamovit, Marie Joi Hosker, Paul Kaplan, Gary Kerschner, Nick Kozak, Sara Lawrence-Lightfoot, Patricia Lindberg, Linda Nathan, Caleb Neelon, Sharon Randolph, Marilyn Rogers, Bonnie Sands, Steve Seidel, Judy Seaton, David Seaton, Carly Simon, Lissa Soep, Robert Stewart, Bill Strickland, Maura Tighe, Jamie Ullrich, David Valdes, Liza Voll, and Jere Williams. Thank you all for your contributions to this book and for all that you make possible. And thanks always to and for Will.

INTRODUCTION

"We seek no fame, we seek no glory, this is just art to tell our story!"

Photograph by the artist, Temp (1987)

"It gets them in the door."

"There is no greater predictor for failure in life than success in high school." Legend has it that the great writer and bon vivant Truman Capote (of *Breakfast at Tiffany's* fame) coined these disparaging words. Capote, who left high school at 17, is one of the many famous people whose alternate roads to success (often in the arts) are celebrated in casual conversation or catalogued in Internet listings such as "Celebrity Dropouts" or "Famous High School Dropouts."[1] These collections boast writers and Mensa geniuses along with superstars in the entertainment industry.

While the lists affirm what young adults who dropped out of high school seem to know—that they were not inadequate losers incapable of succeeding—the roster of impressive names obscures the reality looming for the vast majority of students who choose to leave school. High school dropouts are far more likely to be unemployed and, if employed, to earn less than their peers who graduate. Their chances are increased for poverty, public assistance, and time in prison. And they are more likely to be divorced, in poor health, and single parents of children who will similarly go on to drop out of school. If they had it to do again, most high school dropouts would have stayed in school.[2]

On average, one-fourth of the students who are currently enrolled in our high schools will not graduate. When it comes to minority students (African American, Latino, or Native American), that percentage reaches nearly one-half. The intellectual and financial resources of educational leaders, government, nonprofits, private foundations, social entrepreneurs, and research institutions have been marshaled to face the daunting task of turning around what are called "dropout factories," high schools with attrition rates of more than 60%.[3] Without contest, our alarming high school dropout rate is the most urgent problem facing school reformers on the local and national level. In the pages that follow, I argue that increasing opportunities for arts education in the high school curriculum will help to save the day.

Almost every high school student enters 9th grade with the intention not only of graduating, but also of pursuing postsecondary education. But somewhere along the way too many become detached and lose sight of their goals. What goes wrong? Young adults who have dropped out of high school tell us that, among factors that range from familial demands to peer pressure, their top reason for leaving was that high school was "boring"; "nothing I was interested in"; "the teacher just stood in the front of the room and

3

just talked and didn't really like involve you." The courses, these individuals report, did not seem relevant to their present or future lives.[4]

A lack of interest and relevance erodes the energy and incentive needed to leave your house and go to school. And the more days skipped, the more nights of homework undone, the steeper the climb back into the day-to-day life of school. Absenteeism is not only a prominent indicator of the level or lack of student engagement, it has also been identified as a high-risk marker of a student's likelihood for dropping out.[5] Students vote with their feet, and they are exiting left and right.

High engagement, teacher attention, and increased attendance have long been positively associated with the arts. Dedicated high school students tell us that arts learning inspires passion and engagement on their part and on the part of their teachers. It also inspires industrious hard work that permeates their lives at school.[6] An arts teacher at a public high school reports that "Individual students have told me they come to school for the arts, even if they dread Engineering, Spanish, or Math. It gets them in the door and makes them feel good about themselves."[7]

Recent dropout interventions include quick responses to markers of risk (often apparent in elementary and middle school) such as absenteeism, behavior change, and course failure. Increasing state requirements for compulsory attendance (raising the age at which students are permitted to drop out from 16 to 18) puts higher stakes on leaving school early. Professional training improves teachers' effectiveness, as does strong leadership support. A variety of pathways to graduation, including online courses and schedules that allow students to work, provide alternative venues, while increased oversight from parents and tutors bolsters individual attention.[8]

Supportive strategies such as these are happily meeting with measurable success, but they do not directly address the reported lack of interest and relevance in the subject matter of high school classes. We must consider content along with presentation as we seek to increase the draw of the mainstream courses these students reject. In doing so, it makes sense to turn for remediation to subject areas that give meaning to so many students' lives at school. The time is now, I suggest, to feature rather than to exclude the compelling arenas of drama, music, visual arts, and dance. And this suggestion is not without precedence.

A recent research study, *Staying in School*, reports that in low-performing schools in New York City, when the arts were included, students more frequently attended school on a daily basis, and furthermore, they stayed to graduate.

An analysis of 200 New York City schools over a 2-year period demonstrated that graduation rates were in the top third in those schools providing the most access to and the greatest resources for arts education, while those in the bottom third provided the least. The report concludes with the recommendation that an increase in students' access to arts instruction and experience would improve school life and elevate graduation rates nationwide.[9]

Researchers and educators have observed the power of the arts to enrich school culture and to engage a diverse range of students. From the stellar student who wants to round out her applications to college, to every student who longs to express personal fears and dreams, to the disenfranchised adolescent who admires the image of the artist as outsider. These students come to and for art classes and they stay in school for the rest. And we have yet to mention those individuals with serious aspirations for careers in the arts.

What in particular about the arts captures the attention and dedication of so many young people? That question has driven much of my prior work and is the subject of the work at hand.[10] I intend to provide the reader (the high school student, concerned parent, school administrator, teacher, arts education advocate, and/or policymaker) with the necessary information and perspective with which to argue for a prominent place for the arts in the reformation of high school curriculum.

My discussions benefit not only from prior research but also from recent observations, interviews, and surveys drawn from high school students and teachers of the arts in independent (day and boarding), public, charter, and pilot high school settings. On this account, I have been able to thread my text with the voices of those who are too frequently omitted from the great stage of educational reform: the students and teachers who are the leading players in the drama. While my advocate's voice offers cadence, it is they who articulate best what is compelling about the arts for young people at this particular, important, and, for many, perilous juncture in their lives.

I hope what we uncover here will assist mainstream educational reformers in their rescue of the American high school. Surely arts education advocates will find affirmation and fodder in the pages that follow. But this book also aims to serve those who have yet to consider the importance of the arts in our children's education. In sum, persuasion and change are the objectives of the broader work. As for the balance of my introduction, I set the stage for later discussions by providing briefly: 1) historical context for high schools and arts education; 2) developmental context for students and the arts; and 3) an overview of the order and content of the chapters that follow.

History: High Schools and Art

Whatever the educational venue, questions emerge from and inform daily practice. In the case of the public high school a deceptively simple query persists: "What is it for?" Academically, is its purpose to prepare able students who have or can find the financial resources to go to college? Realistically, is it meant to ready for success those who will immediately enter the workforce? Idealistically, should it provide all students with equal skills and opportunity to participate in a democratic society? Cynically, is it a holding ground or warehouse for possible offenders we'd like to keep off the street?

The questions that attend to the education of adolescents (individuals transitioning to adulthood) challenge our resources and reflect our various perspectives on youth (from idealization to criminalization). Inscribed as they are in the fiber of these institutions, these queries have charted the direction and growth of high schools in the United States. Suggesting an overlooked affinity, the other educational scenario in which the issue of purpose persists is the arena of the arts. Where they have reserved a secure place in the curriculum for subjects like math and science, educators and administrators throughout time have balanced the arts on that metaphoric budget chopping block and asked repeatedly, "Yes, but what are they for?"

Experientially, do they provide tools with which students can better see and represent the world? Behaviorally, do they provide opportunities for the release of otherwise intrusive emotions (and perhaps even excess energy) in a safe and contained environment? Academically, do they encourage habits of learning such as perseverance and self-discipline? Culturally, do they help students appreciate the great works of art that have survived over time?

When public high schools (the first private high school was founded in 1635) were founded in the early 19th century, their numbers were few and their purpose was clear: to ready elite students (young men) for their college-bound futures. Course content necessarily contained a strong foundation in classical academics. With regard to the arts, the study of drawing was thought to help develop more graceful handwriting and to awaken observational skills. This approach was vigorously nonexpressive: "Art was not a subject for release of the imagination, but a means of directing the powers of observation, forcing the student to record what he saw."[11]

By the latter part of that century, public high schools began to increase in numbers and to open their doors more broadly. They would now serve young women in search of teaching careers and working-class youth eager to gain marketable skills for a burgeoning industrial revolution. In this context, visual arts education would feature techniques of draftsmanship to help new immigrants find jobs. Music would be taught as a useful resource for worshippers in church. And the study of aesthetics (appreciation of art and beauty) would help to awaken the sensitivities and judgment of Americans who had hitherto thought of themselves as unartistic and pragmatic. In this regard, they compared sorrily to Europeans, who were viewed as cultivated connoisseurs of fine art. "America's material prosperity," arts education historian Diane Korzenik explains, "depended on all people becoming artistic."[12]

By the late 19th and early 20th centuries, Americans were vigorously "becoming artistic." Overcoming their arts-related insecurities, they were building museums and concert halls designed to equal those in Europe. On the high school front, serving an increasingly diverse population, separate high schools evolved alternately for academic (precollegiate) or vocational training (in which academic courses were part but not the focus of the curriculum). Arts curriculum–wise, the work of Arthur Wesley Dow, a leading figure in the American Arts and Crafts revival, held sway. His 1899 book on composition was used in the public schools and emphasized the aim even of experiential art activities to be the systematic intellectual development of aesthetic appreciation.[13]

By the turn of the 20th century, egalitarian progressive educators eschewed the inequalities of vocational versus academic learning and looked beyond career outcome to more general educational objectives. The new perspective was that all high school students (the minority who were destined for college, the majority who were headed for trades, and everyone in between) should receive the same education—albeit potentially more accessible than demanding. General studies (preparation for life and citizenship rather than for either college or technical trades) began to edge out academic or career disciplines.[14] A set of Cardinal Principles (1918) was set out for secondary education, with room in the curriculum for music, art, and drama under the principle of "Worthy Use of Leisure."[15] These were the days when educators were to speak of nurturing the "whole child" and attending to the development of such nonquantifiable virtues as inquisitiveness and social responsibility.

Philosopher and educator John Dewey argued for experiential art activities as opportunities for more fully understanding the world. He wrote, "If all meanings could be adequately expressed by words, the arts of painting and music would not exist."[16] Concepts like imagination, creativity, and self-expression proudly entered the educational conversation. And even at the high school level (where arts courses were self-selected and maintained an emphasis on technical skills), arts learning was respected as a means to develop independent thinkers who could construct and understand universal truths.

Out of this context, influential art educator Viktor Lowenfeld would advocate active hands-on learning in the visual arts and posit a set of artistic stages from the early scribbles of preschool children to the age of decision (whether to abandon or continue drawing) for high school students.[17] Drawing on the modernist quest for freedom from traditional constraints, high school art students in the progressive tradition were encouraged to create for themselves and not to consider, either on their own or in terms of their developing efforts, the work of famous artists of the past and present.[18]

These progressive views would be overturned in the next few decades by a more cognitive view of arts learning (seeing the arts as more about thinking than feeling) and a view of the different arts arenas as serious disciplinary domains of thought.[19] From a view of the child as artist (a maker of art), we moved to a view of the student connoisseur as an informed patron (appreciator) of the arts.

The turn in attitudes had been stimulated by the embarrassing news that the Russians in 1957 (ahead of the United States) had succeeded in the first launching of an artificial satellite. Responsibility for this failure of course fell to the schools. Were there no highly trained creative scientists coming out of our educational system? In order to correct this situation, there was a push for academic excellence, with a greater emphasis on science and math and less attention to humanistic subjects, perhaps especially the several disciplines of the arts.

Conversations about the emotional value of arts in the curriculum would lose favor in the call for a more substantive approach to teaching and learning. In order to challenge and prime potential achievers, there would be separate tracking (under the same school roof) of high school students of promise and those with lesser potential. But how would the difference be determined and at what ethical cost? Were socioeconomic strata and racial bias silent differentials in the decision as to which students were tracked for Honors or Advanced Placement and which for a more general non-college-bound program? These questions have persisted through the late 20th century and its recent turn. What is high school for? Who is it meant to serve? If everyone, and in large numbers, then how? And what place if any is there for learning in the arts?

In 1984, when renowned educator Ted Sizer wrote his groundbreaking text, *Horace's Compromise: The Dilemma of the American High School*,[20] he argued that in spite of the wide diversity of adolescent personalities and needs, high school curriculum seemed to hold across the lines of location (urban, suburban, rural) and class (socioeconomic). Wherever he found the high schools he studied in the late 1970s, there was a constant push for "coverage" and "attendance." Courses were about the breadth of content they could provide, and progress up the ladder from freshman to senior relied on students showing up. Overall, Sizer likened high schools to supermarkets where students were rushing in predictable patterns collecting items for their cart "the faster the better."

The courses on the shelves that Sizer's high school shoppers were instructed to select were pretty much what they are today: English, social studies, mathematics, science, and foreign language. [21] And if you were lucky, in the specialty section, you might find some offerings in visual arts and music. But beyond the flurry of alternative charter and pilot schools (some of which focus on the arts), the 21st century has seen budget cuts reduce or eliminate serious instruction in any or all of the arts. Along with a streamlining of offerings, and perhaps at greatest peril, the current climate has taken to heart the sharp-edged, nonnegotiable judgment of standardized testing.[22] It is fair to say that high-stakes testing now holds center stage, determining the future not only of individual students, but also of teachers and classrooms and schools themselves.

Arts education has been pushed so far to the margins that desperate advocates have fought for a place at the head table by arguing that arts learning even helps to increase student performance on non-arts–related standardized tests.[23] It has been shown that across all kinds of variables, students who study the arts do better on their SATs than those who don't. In fact, the longer they study the arts, the better students seem to do. The problem is that it is hard, even with strong correlations, to demonstrate that it is arts learning itself that has caused the improvement. For example, excellent schools tend to include arts education, and since those schools are excellent, they might also be providing superior instruction in the subjects being tested.

These considerations, so extraneous and removed from the powerful learning that the arts provide, are a symptom of the time. The paint is fresh on monochromatic backdrops of win or lose in which the quality and value of student learning, teacher skills, administrative acumen, and school culture are determined by performance on standardized tests. The checkout lane in Sizer's supermarket has taken on ominous proportions.

Development: Children and Art

The head of a progressive secondary school that emphasizes the arts explains his understanding that all people fundamentally are drawn to art: "I think the desire to make art has to be ruined and it frequently is." The director of a veteran after-school community arts program believes that the arts provide the ground for our very first emotional and intellectual experience: "We are brought into this world and mothers instinctively run and sing with their children and clap with and for them." When we take away the arts, this advocate declares, children actively miss some "fundamental" part of their lives.

Certainly it is true that all children come to school with the ability to make art. Five-year-olds draw images as wildly expressive as the modernist art you can find in a museum. They sing songs of their own design and dance along with great rhythm and pace. In the preschool pretend play corner, you see young children playing roles with the imagination and intensity of mature actors. "That's not what the mother would do," one 4-year-old will critique another who is jumping up and down.

The young child comes to school overflowing with artistry, effectively if unknowingly breaking artistic conventions and rules of language and action with an apparently innate ability to create metaphor and meaning. "I'm melting," the 5-year-old will tell you of her descent from a high place to the floor. At age 8, she will consider that allusion a mistake.

The arts are a seamless ingredient in messy preschool learning. But as we introduce students to the clear-cut requirements of subjects like reading and math (and this seems to be happening at earlier ages), we inadvertently devalue their artistic expression. "Pictures are fine, but soon you will learn to write and read the stories they tell." Pretend play and music stations give way to desks and books. Making art, that innate activity, becomes something you do with a special teacher usually no more than once a week.

If the subtle devaluation of the arts is not clear to 12-year-old children (the age at which most kids will tell you they are or more frequently that they are not artists), it is certainly apparent to high school students who see the arts relegated to extracurricular activity or demeaned as gut courses worthy only of the most minimal requirements. In spite of their place in a culture that is everywhere layered with visual, musical, and theatrical images, high school students are receiving the message that the arts are of no consequence—not worth much of your time in school.

This attitude speaks against the reality of the world that adolescents experience, and it speaks against whatever intuitive artistic predilection they may retain from early childhood. A 9th-grader in an arts-based high school believes that "everybody is an artist—all people have artistic ability," and for her own part, "Even as a child I knew this modern world with so many rules was stifling, art comes naturally, the title of artist should too."

Approximately 40 out of the 50 states have some kind of an arts requirement (school statistics are not as easy to gather as one might think) of a half or full credit (equivalent to a semester or year of coursework).[24] But a number of these states require the arts only of college-bound high school students and/or indicate that the requirement can alternately be filled by study in foreign language, vocational education, computers, speech and debate, and so on. Alarmed by these "substitutes," the National Arts Education Association has issued the statement: "For purposes of developing curricular areas, we define the fine arts as consisting of the visual arts, dance, music, and theater."[25]

The arts are regarded as perpetual outsiders, struggling to gain stable ground or even just to get their foot in the door of prioritized curriculum. Perhaps it is true that their outsider status aligns the arts with those students who feel estranged or are thinking of leaving or have left high school. For certain, the impressive stories of success at community art centers that work with students who have dropped out of school would point to a connection. Students at risk across a number of variables find personal support and opportunities for success in these safe havens for teaching and learning in the arts.[26]

The devaluation of the arts in schools and the consequent absence of steady sequential (from beginner to advanced) arts learning have taken their toll on artistic development throughout the life span. Overall, many of us have observed students' artistic development as a nonlinear trajectory best described as a U-curve. On account of the vibrant artistlike expressivity of young children's drawings, 5-year-olds occupy the left peak of the U and professional artists the other.

Rather than developing in a straight line across the top of the U (from those early artistic triumphs to the mature state of the professional artist), most children between the ages of 8 and 12 appear to fall into the trough of the U. That is to say, their drawings share few if any of the expressive qualities of the work of professional artists. There has been an apparent decline from early artistic freedom to tight conventional stick-figure renderings. Indeed, children at this age often add words of explanation to their drawings, certain that the images themselves will never tell the story.[27]

There is much debate as to why some children pull themselves together, recover the excitement of early efforts, and proceed in their development up the steep curve to the territory of artist-adolescents and sometimes even to that of professional artists. Some argue that it is talent; others that it is persistence; and still others that those students who persevere in making art attend schools or after-school programs where their artistic efforts are supported. In these settings, students are encouraged to develop their artistry and to have for life a facility (if not a marketable talent) to draw or sing or act out an idea or emotion. By adolescence, in the current scene, too many students declare that they are "done" with art-making. "We're not good at it anyways."

I hold with those who believe that the exit from art-making is not based on a lack of pleasure with the experience but on dwindling opportunity for development (the arts are taught less frequently in later grades and into high school than in the beginning years of school) and a sense that the arts do not matter in the adult world (as reflected by the decline in resource and instruction). No matter how difficult it may be for a student, he or she is not likely or allowed to say, "I'm done with math." Why should it be possible with regard to the arts? Happily, there is evidence that the early passion and facility can be reawakened in youth or adulthood[28] and are often actively sought out by older adults.[29] If, as that headmaster said, "the desire to make art has to be ruined," these older adults demonstrate that it can be resurrected.

When it comes to students of high school age, we have a disjuncture. Adolescents are cognitively at the ready to create and deconstruct the verbal metaphors that underlie a poem,[30] and they are in close touch with the vibrant emotions that fuel the broader range of art-making and appreciation. But high schools, ignoring the readiness of their students to engage deeply with arts learning, have taken the arts off the daily menu of most students' courses. This omission challenges the futures of cultural institutions like art museums, theaters, and concert halls. A population uneducated in the arts will not pursue them in their lives beyond school.

Moreover, and this is the concern of the work at hand, the omission of the arts in the high school curriculum deprives students of learning that is well aligned with their personal needs and interests, learning that will equip them with modes of self-discovery and expression, learning that gives them a reason to attend and to stay in school. And, most important, learning that other subjects simply do not provide. As a high school freshman explained:

> I love doing art, I love dancing, I love creative writing. I HAVE to dance
> and do art. When I'm dead and gone, sprinkled hopefully in the ocean or
> another place of full-blown cliché, the people I love will die and all that
> will remain is either the materialistic crap that I have collected or the
> work of my brain. I hope that the work of my brain lasts longer. I know
> that by doing art you have achievements, you have prospect, and you
> have an escape—an adrenaline rush amid this boring world.

Order: Chapters and Content

In my guide to arts education advocacy, *Why Our Schools Need the Arts,* I posit five features of the arts that make them unique among school subjects and 10 specific and invaluable spheres of learning that emerge therefrom. This text is organized around these qualities and learning outcomes situated within the high school context and threaded with rich accounts from high school students and teachers of the arts.

With this in mind, I devote a chapter each to:

1. Tangible Product (the something that we can see or touch or hear that we call art) and its attendant learning outcomes of Imagination (the ability to see beyond the given) and Agency (the realization of self-capacity).
2. A Focus on Emotion (art's unique association with the world of feeling) and the outcomes of Expression (as recognition/ articulation of one's own feelings) and Empathy (as recognition/ understanding of the feelings of another).
3. Ambiguity (art's intentional delivery of multiple meanings) and the resultant facilities of Interpretation (meaning-making that includes the realization that different understandings can be equally valid) and Respect (as attention to and appreciation for others' perspectives).
4. Process Orientation (art's exemplary focus on the doing, making, dancing, singing, etc.) and the attendant skills of Inquiry (the ability to ask real questions) and Reflection (close and purposeful assessment of progress). And last,
5. Connection (art's timeless manifestation of our shared humanity) and the relevant outcomes of: Engagement (a passionate attachment to the work at hand and to other human beings who are similarly engaged), and Responsibility (a resolve to make a positive difference in our communities and the world).

Even as high school dropouts found them lacking from the subjects they were taught, interest and relevance are the very qualities that attract high school students to the arts. Drawing on the discussions in previous chapters, in a final chapter, I summarize the specific ways in which the arts evoke interest for and are relevant to high school students and make a final call for increased curricular inclusion. It is my hope that what we uncover here will assist educational reformers in their efforts to help more high school students stay in school and graduate. The human potential that fuels the arts can help transform "low-performing" high schools into hopeful arenas that enable students who have been placed at risk to assume their rightful place of promise.

CHAPTER 1

TANGIBLE PRODUCT

Senior Visual Arts Project in a Gallery Exhibit

Photograph by the artist, Kandace Cook

"The idea that I can create these things . . . "

In the musical *Sunday in the Park with George,* the painter Georges Seurat, through the lyrics and music of Steven Sondheim, explains art-making with a simple reverent phrase, "Look I made a hat, where there never was a hat."[1] It may be a visual image, assemblage, sculpture, dance performance, or original poem or song. But in the arts, there is always an entity that is created, something that was not there before the artist painted, assembled, sculpted, danced, or wrote it. Betty Blayton-Taylor, artist and founder of the Children's Art Carnival in Harlem, described art-making as "turning our thoughts into things."[2] And whether the resultant "things" can be seen or heard or touched or watched or even just talked about, there is in mind or actuality a tangible product that inspires and fulfills the artistic process, a product conceived and constructed by the maker of art.

Surely the geometry proofs set out by the math teacher for students to solve or the science experiments designated for students to perform have a material aspect—a something you complete and turn in as assigned. And you can make that submission tidy or messy, accurate or vague, and loaded with or seriously lacking right actions and/or answers. Either way, the assignment is prescribed by the teacher, not invented by the student, and the range of options for completion lie within the boundaries of the task's and the teacher's expectations. In short, there is little room within most non-arts class assignments for an imaginative alternative or a personal statement.

If the class is asked to perform an experiment exploring the corrosive nature of oxidation, a student will not be rewarded for submitting a personal poem on metallic decay in lieu of the lab report. It is obviously extremely important for students to learn the scientific method and the ways to apply postulates and theorems to the solution of a geometry proof. But in the manifestation or demonstration of that learning, we see a fundamental difference from learning in the arts.

Unlike the experiment or the proof, from inception to completion, the tangible product that students create in arts classes is of their own design. And this is true even when there are creative constraints such as specified materials in visual arts or suggested themes in music, dance, or drama. The unique composition of the tangible product reflects the imagination and personal agency of its maker.

Imagination: What If

Imagination, that facility so rightly associated with the arts, is the ability to think beyond the given, to consider "what if." Personal agency is the realization of one's own ability to do that and more, to bring the "what if" into being, to make a difference, to "matter." In the great journey from childhood to adulthood, these two facilities—imagining a future determined by your decisions and actions, and confidence in your ability to affect these ends—are of the utmost importance.[3]

A sophomore who considers himself "not a full-fledged artist but one who is willing to learn more which I think all artists are" told me, "I think of myself as an artist because of how I see things. I never see things for what they are but for what they can be. I see a table and think, 'how would it look on its side or if somebody were hiding behind it?'" With this ability to see beyond the given, David experiences a sense of personal power: "It's so beautiful seeing beyond what is there."

Adults who have dropped out of high school report that a lack of ownership of their work alienated them from assignments. They "complained [that] teachers just told them what to do without involving them in the lesson."[4] This sentiment was shared by an academically successful senior in an East Coast boarding school: "In the other classes, you put one foot in front of the other. 'Here is the test, do the bare minimum needed to get the highest grade.' I put in a higher personal standard for art than for any other class." Another senior, this one in a West Coast public high school, concurs to the extreme:

> Art is the class, where you get to think for yourself without people telling you what to do. . . . In other classes like geometry and science, you're stuck with a curriculum the teacher gets to choose, and you can't do anything about it. It's a dictatorship in a way. "I have this stuff to teach you, and I am going to force you upon it, and you can't do anything about it. Learn or fail," that's the attitude I get from all of my academic classes besides art.

Exploring the difference between arts and non-arts classes, I asked an experienced theater teacher how he thinks his high school–aged students would distinguish his teaching style. "I would hope that they would say we learn together." He explains how he sets the stage for such collaborative learning:

My approach to teaching has always been a simple one. Let the students lead the way. Encourage them to be skeptical of what you are telling them and make you prove what you are espousing. Avoid at all times the natural tendency to seek approval from you. And most importantly, treat them all as potentially future colleagues.

This community-based teacher aims to teach his students to "be independent and critical thinkers": If students "don't feel a personal ownership of the tenants I have taught them, if they aim to get things right as opposed to expressing their true selves, I have failed them."

An urban school-based high school theater teacher echoed the lesson of agency and ownership:

The primary lesson I strive for is ownership of one's work. Taking responsibility for one's choices and knowing one's own potential is key to this age group. Especially with such a strong population of students who may not be getting strong identity-building experiences outside of school, I focus on what each student does that shows initiative and self-direction. For example, I chart students' grades based clearly on the quality of their work *and* their ability to navigate their own choices. Do they pass in assignments on time? Do they choose to wear appropriate clothing? Do they decide to read the entire play instead of just their scene? Each aspect of the student's work is framed as a choice he/she can make that will either aid their understanding of the lesson, or diminish it.

How might the overall experience of those students who dropped out of school have benefited from the opportunities for ownership (as a sense of personal agency) that the arts present?

Through the works of art that they create on their own, students gain a broader and more nuanced understanding of what it is to learn. Right answers are by their very nature replicable. The tangible products created through art are as intrinsically singular. A senior in a charter high school said of her work in the visual arts, "I love that art is unique and cannot be duplicated. Sure, ideas can be recycled and represented and concepts will never cease to reappear. But the image, the mere image itself that I create, can never be repeated."

The hat. The drawing. The dramatic rendering. These tangible imprints of student effort reflect their makers' imaginations—their personal considerations of what if. Tenth-grader David said that "creativity is imagination plus belief: wearing a pot lid as a hat is imagination; the belief is that it doesn't look bad as a hat." Where would your imagination and belief take you if you were invited to wrap your secrets in a bundle of clay? That challenging assignment is described in the teaching memoir of visual artist and teacher Richard Olsen. He began the exercise with this intriguing "what if":

> I held up a ball of clay. "What do you think about this?" I asked.
> "Nothing . . . just a ball of clay" was the response.
> "What if I told you that inside this ball was the principal's deepest darkest secret; would that change how you looked at it?"
> The kids laughed and, imagining what it might be, agreed that somehow the ball of clay would change. We then talked about how what we know or think about something can affect how we relate to it.[5]

Olsen raises the same question of context ("how what we know or think about something can affect how we relate to it") posed by philosopher Nelson Goodman in his classic essay, *When Is Art?* Not what is art, but when. If a stone is lying in a driveway, do you look at it twice, or at all? But what if that stone is put on a pedestal in an art gallery? Do you see it more fully, even noticing small details of its composition? Does its placement in the museum or your careful attention change the status of that stone, maybe even from something of no meaning to a work of art?[6]

The assignment is to write about a teenager like me. But what if she lives somewhere else? Can I imagine a world very different from mine? How will I give it detail and life? Will she deal with the same problems that I do, or will her world be very different? How different? Unlike the prescribed and fixed frameworks of many assignments in non-arts classes, the challenges that teachers present in arts classrooms are there for students to reframe, reassemble, and redefine.

The student's autonomy in creating his or her own world can be exhilarating for the adolescent who feels the "stress" (a word frequently used to distinguish between non-arts and arts classrooms) of an environment with prescribed and high-stakes expectations. A 9th-grader tells me that "The art teachers at my school seem a lot less stressed than the other teachers . . . the atmosphere is a lot easier to learn in." Michael, a veteran high school ceramics teacher, explains:

> In my classroom students are given an opportunity to explore many different options or solutions to the problems presented. In most other classes they are simply being fed information and given very few options. My classroom is a place where conversation replaces the lecture format.

Making the stress versus non-stress point, he goes on,

> The atmosphere within my room is relaxed, with music playing and
> students working at their own pace rather than artificial, teacher-
> imposed deadlines. This approach is not without its dangers, but most
> students enjoy the freedom and rise to the occasion.

The music teacher who asks the young pianist to close her eyes before she plays and imagine what it will sound like. The drama teacher who asks two students to create a dialogue between a policeman and a young man who has been wrongly arrested. Moving as if your body were made of wood, painting images of chairs "as if" they were alive and capable of emotion. The arts offer students the opportunity to create something new and in that act of making not only to think beyond the boundaries and the lines but also to acknowledge one's power to do so. One senior explained to me, "I have learned . . . how to tackle a problem very many ways and in art the idea of a box is broken and you can pretty much do anything you want."

High school–aged students are intellectually ready and able for the sort of abstract thinking that the arts inspire—those considerations of time and possibility that hover beyond the here and now.[7] Michael explains that the malleable boundaries of "making and looking at art are important for the adolescent's developing mind. It forces them to think differently and become critical thinkers."

Critical thinking is essential to the process of making good decisions. But it takes confidence to see beyond the given, the box, the stress of day-to-day demands. Opportunities to imagine "what if" enable high school students to hone the skills they need to consider their own futures and the worlds on which they want to have impact. A disgruntled high school freshman explained:

> Art teachers at my school don't force things upon you. They give you an
> idea and leave it in the open for you to develop off of. Art teachers teach
> the things students need most—critical thinking. All of my other classes
> force things upon you and you have to take exactly what they give you.
> You can't use your imagination and build something else.

It is not just in the making of art that you use your imagination to conceive and create something else; imagination is also involved in perceiving and appreciating works of art created by others. The great educational philosopher Maxine Greene asserts, "It is my conviction that informed engagements with the several arts is the most likely mode of releasing our students' (or any person's) imaginative capacity and giving it play."[8]

Looking at a work of art in a museum, students can imagine themselves as one of the subjects of the painting or as the artist who created it. They might wonder what they would have named the painting had they made it themselves. What of my possessions would be there with me if I were the subject of this portrait? Sitting in the audience of a theatrical performance, students can imagine themselves as the characters in the play—or the actors onstage—considering the choices being made "as if" they were their own.

A resonant example (a favorite of mine) comes from Dollie McLean, founding executive director of the Artists Collective in Hartford, Connecticut. The Collective is a community art center with an African/Caribbean American focus that has served as a safe haven of success for numerous adolescents who have given up on or been given up on by schools. Mrs. McLean speaks to the power of performance to inspire "what if," helping youth to consider the alternative of hours in practice rooms over their time on the street:

> That's how our kids need to get high—off that adrenaline that's so natural and . . . when you're getting ready to do something and all of your parents are sitting outside and your friends and the boys from the hood—they've all come. I heard a few of them [in the audience]. I was sitting behind some of them. They said, "I can do that." I leaned over and said, "Yes, yes, you could."[9]

The arts awaken possibilities in student thinking that liberate heart and mind and, most importantly, assert one's personal potential, agency, or power. A high school music teacher wants her students "to value their individuality and to respect their final product," and to "help them see the value of sharing their work with others." "I can do that," one might say from the audience. "You did that!" resounds for the performers in the audience's applause. As if he'd heard Dollie McLean's choice of high, a 9th-grader said of his work:

> All of the art I do is special to me because it is a place where I have all the control, the world of my art is mine and my own so when I can be in my world, it is a moment of true ecstasy (no drugs involved).

Agency: I Matter

From the creation or consideration of that tangible product that is a work of art, students experience the profound, essential, and relevant learning outcome: I make a difference. If I decide that angel represents death, the meaning that I make out of the painting that I'm viewing (not a prescribed, definite, or right explanation) is transformed. I imagine the painting I am creating as a fierce commentary on HIV. My addition of shadows and dark angles can turn the image into what I imagine.

I make the artistic decisions that realize my artistic intentions and perceptions. My imagining and mattering are visible both in the tangible product that is my work of art and in the meaning I make out of another's work of art. An East Coast 9th-grader with little experience in the visual arts put it as simply as Sondheim: "I created a small abstract drawing. I enjoyed having complete creative control over what I was doing."

A senior dedicated to the arts expanded, "The most important thing about the art I make is that it's mine and though people give their comments, it's ultimately up to me, my inner thoughts and insanities." A veteran music teacher explained the variety of self-competency or agency that learning in music provides:

Self-esteem, a critical part of teenage development, can be addressed through the study of music. Measurable and concrete goals are achieved through hard work, audience reaction/approval, and personal/individual achievements versus competing in the classroom. This all can add up to developing a healthy self-esteem in a music student.

These comments and perceptions are so very far from what the adults who had dropped out were saying about their experience of high school: "a lack of connection to the school environment; a perception that school is boring; feeling unmotivated."[10] The freedom to create something of one's own making ("to pretty much do anything you want") in the setting of the arts classroom is an academic and cognitive freedom. It does not align with the excess of freedom several students who dropped out cited as one of the reasons they left:

Once you get in high school, it's more like you have more freedom. In middle school, you have to go to your next class or they are going to get you. In high school, if you don't go to class there isn't anyone who is going to get you. You just do your own thing.[11]

Students get themselves to the arts classroom and recognize the importance of their participation. As one high school junior told me, "If I'm missing from my French class, I can get the assignment. If I don't show for art, I'm in trouble." The combination of imagination (what if) and personal agency (I matter) sets the stage for a sense of possibility and self-determination. In a study of schools that focus on the arts, administrators reported that students came early to school before class and stayed late after rehearsals, apparently unable to separate from the commitment and hard work that motivated them through the day.[12]

If my use of black in this image transforms the whole, if my high-stepping leap adds intrigue to the power of the dance, how much can my personal decisions change the course of events in my singular life and in the larger world? Maxine Greene has taught us about the power of the arts to awaken students to new understandings of their individual and shared worlds and to see themselves as agents of change: "We want to enable all sorts of young people to realize that they have the right to find works of art meaningful against their own lived lives." And if we do, "Communities of the wide-awake may take shape, even in the corridors of schools."[13]

Richard Olsen describes this sort of wide-awake action on the part of one of his students who used her art to respond to a change in tenor in the overall school environment. Olsen tells us that the school had become "another modernist institution dedicated to high test scores and uninformed practice. What it gained in order and accountability, it lost in complexity and passion":

> One year, things were particularly sharp. Posters denouncing new rules began to appear in the halls (and be immediately taken down by the administration in a kind of cat and mouse game). Kids gathered among themselves and talked about how "fascist" everything had become.
>
> One of my students began a new work. Usually, her pieces were lyrical depictions of girls and filled with bright colors. This one was different. Restricting her pallet to the school colors, students were portrayed as puppets under the control of the administration. The school slogans were painted in their original font, but had been altered to tell kids "not to think." Parts of the painting had been burned away. The whole piece was draped in chains.
>
> Coming to school one morning and seeing it in the school gallery, the new principal was not pleased. I was removed from class and taken to task for allowing it to be shown. Scores of kids meanwhile had gathered around the work, both shocked and exhilarated by it. To remove it at that point would only prove the correctness of its critique. It was thus—for the time being—allowed to stay. Most amazingly, regular lessons had to be postponed, as all the kids were talking about the painting and the issues it raised. For the first time, kids and teachers

collectively debated what the school had become, with the teachers on the defensive. That the administration ultimately weathered the storm didn't distract from the significance of the event itself.[14]

This story of gallery-based protest may not seem the ideal tale to tell when advocating for the inclusion of arts in the menu of courses we require of high school students. Many principals would prefer that such interruptions be avoided. But it stands as a vivid example of the art object's ability to speak in ways that words cannot and to engage and activate students in the world around them. Better for this young woman to be heard than for her to turn her back on her school. An art happening like the one described here is imbued with the kind of caring for the school community that will keep a student working through dialogue toward change rather than walking away in frustration and despair.

Contemporary artists like Suzanne Lacy have worked over the last 40 years to "produce performances and installations that function as public hearings to advance policy impacting young people."[15] Lacy's installations have awakened public attention and stimulated discourse on issues ranging from teen pregnancy to street violence to personal depression. Demonstrating the power and durability of the artistic product, the videotape of the workshop she produced, *Youth Cops and Videotape,* continues to be used in police training for the Oakland Police Department.

Starting with an installation of more than 200 parked cars on a roof ("The Roof Is on Fire") and including frank conversations among teens and police officers (taped in discourse within and around the vehicles and in subsequent meetings around issues of community unrest), the video portrays honest back-and-forth in which youth and police try to understand each other's points of view.[16] The work features two concepts that are key to art-making and appreciation: 1) the power of listening, attending—the close attention to detail that is developed in learning to make sense through and of a work of art; and 2) the power of a question, that if you begin with a question—as works of art do—instead of a predictable assumption about the "other," anything is possible.

One way that we experience the humanity of a work of art is through our awareness of the thought and touch of the artist who has created it. The tangible product can last for centuries (some are destroyed in a moment even as part of the creation) and tell a very different story to a current generation than to one past. But the conversation continues and rings true because of the timeless issues embodied and addressed in the work. We need to make room for the human conversation to which arts learning entitles our students, the one imprinted on the work and the one that transpires in the live conversations that enrich and distinguish arts classrooms.

An adult who dropped out of high school was wistful: "If they related to me more and understood what at this point in time, my life was . . . what I was going through, where I lived, where I came from. Who knows?"[17] Reading between the lines of these regretful former students, one hears, "If only these places had been more human." Arts education can do that for our high schools. From the work of art itself to the issues that inform making and appreciating, arts classrooms feature human connection and individual attention.

We know from recent successes in diminishing the dropout rate in several states that the involvement of parents and tutors, providing ears to listen and strategies for assistance, makes an enormous difference to students at risk of leaving school.[18] The kind of individual attention that says, "I see you and want to know what you need." A veteran high school arts teacher explains how he sets up his classroom for individual development:

> Allow them to explore and discover. Don't tell them what to do or how to do it, but instead, allow them to discover on their own. This may call for extreme patience on the part of the teacher, but kids learn by doing. One cannot produce art by teaching a group to do it one way (factory art). I learned at a very early age that students yield better results when they have opportunities to develop individually. I try to provide an environment that allows them to feel safe, and nurtured. The class must have a foundation of trust and honesty in order for it to be nurturing. The biggest lesson that I learn almost every day is that I, as a teacher, mentor, coach, can be a student as well. I must feel that I can learn something every day from my kids. Whether it is how to teach, coach, or mentor, I must have a purpose to teach every day. Kids, through a creative process, can teach me to be a better teacher and artist.

The individual attention of a ceramics teacher in the high school that non-profit guru Bill Strickland was about to leave made the difference that helped him graduate. Strickland remembers passing by the open door of the ceramics studio and stopping to ask the teacher, Frank Ross, how he did the magic that he was doing. "Come in and I'll show you." And Ross offered Strickland a "cup of coffee"—a small gesture that honored the teenager, the sort of gesture that passes from one adult to another.

Out of that relationship of learning and respect, Strickland gained the courage and portfolio to apply to a place called college, and that educational step forward changed the rest of his life. Now the executive director of the Manchester Craftsmen's Guild in Pittsburgh, Pennsylvania, Strickland passes on the lesson and the model to youth throughout the Pittsburgh area, most of whom have been identified as at risk for failure in school.

The Guild offers free after-school classes with close individual mentorship and pedagogy based on a mutually respectful model of professional training. Strickland enables hundreds of students to find the satisfaction and inspiration inherent in creating the tangible product (originally photographs and ceramics, now also jazz composition) that is a work of art. In gallery exhibitions in which they are expected to answer questions about their work, students at the Guild break through the codes of their neighborhoods to speak to a range of individuals interested in their work.

Furthermore, they learn to speak the speak that they will need to use when addressing admissions officers and then teachers in the colleges Strickland expects them to attend. These interactions transpire against a backdrop of considerable beauty. Situated in a poor and weathered neighborhood, the Guild is housed in a splendid building with lots of glass, adorned within with quilts and other valuable works of art (never vandalized) that Strickland believes tell the students of their worth:

> Hey man, you're worth something. Hey man, I care about you. You're going to college. Your life's going to change. We're going to turn the sunshine on and let it bathe you. Sunshine is free, it doesn't cost nothing. You don't need to be rich to walk in the sun; you can be anybody to walk in the sun.[19]

Indeed, the Guild is well known for its success in encouraging students to finish high school and attend college. While on average only 64% of students in the Pittsburgh public schools graduate in 5 years, Strickland reports that almost all (96%) of the students who attend after-school art classes at the Guild (most of them bussed from and by their schools to the Guild) graduate, and 85% of them go on to college. The program at the Guild has been replicated in other cities, and numerous other community-based programs offer similarly inspirational stories of what arts learning can do for youth who have been placed at risk.[20]

Beyond school walls, in art centers that focus on education, we find young adults (many of whom have been classified as at risk for failure across multiple variables) voting positively with their feet. Students who excel in school, others who have found no success in the arena of school, and still others who want to develop into professional artists self-select to attend these centers of arts learning and stay in attendance year after year, progressing in their arts learning from beginner to advanced.[21]

Of pride to the centers, many students return in later life to teach or create similar venues in their new communities. Studies have shown that out of all after-school activities, students at the highest risk of failure across a number of variables will select arts educational centers and reap the greatest benefits from art-making and performing as well as life skills that serve within and across a range of settings.[22] Our high schools could reach more students than those that find these safe havens for the arts. Our high schools could provide what so many students look elsewhere to find. We need to embrace in schools the beliefs and practices that permeate arts education beyond school walls.

High schools that include the arts, that offer opportunities for students to create and make sense of works of art, set the stage for dedication and engagement across all subjects as well as the courage and perseverance needed to stay in school. Community arts educators believe this and more: that arts learning can save the lives of youth who face risks including low expectations, poverty, illness, and the challenge of difference from race to sexual identity. "You can't teach them algebra," Strickland is quoted as saying, "if they don't want to live."[23]

Beyond Measure

It all begins with the tangible product, whether a painting or piece of writing that I can revisit repeatedly, or a video of a drama or dance performance that happened in the moment. The existence or record of the tangible product allows the student to have repeated interactions with the work, new opportunities to make sense of its meaning and new opportunities to experience the imagination and agency that it reflects. Whether it speaks to the inner struggles or dreams or complaints of the artist, a work of art is singular in its potential to embrace and empower student ideas.

Nonetheless, and especially in this age of count and measure, doubters will dismiss the value of the art product because its achievement cannot be given a quantitative score. Who is to say that the young woman's multimedia public art in the gallery of her school is of equal, more, or less merit than the abstract drawing of the uninitiated 9th-grader, or the dance performance at the Artists Collective in Hartford? The products of art unapologetically defy measurement even as they invite a lively and different kind of conversation around meaning-making, perspective, and a student's place in the world.

While arts education advocates have long railed against the inadequacy of standardized tests as determinations of the "whole" story of student learning, now even those educators who promoted these methods decry the current wave of quantification that is drowning our students and our schools.[24] We have moved from Sizer's benign metaphor of the American high school as a fast-moving supermarket to the shocking mechanistic view of our high schools as dropout factories. There is need for balance and the arts can provide.

We must insist that all our students, those excelling in academic areas and those struggling to stay aboard, have the regular experience of creating something—of imagining what if and realizing a vision. These are opportunities that the arts afford in ways that other subjects do not. Even as we speculate that the arts experience may have implications for students' attachment to and participation in subjects across the board, let us remember the valuable learning that the arts most particularly provide: the chance for all students, regardless of their predilection for or talent in the arts, to feel themselves artists, creating something that was not there before they imagined it or brought it into being.

A high school junior spoke to me of the reach and promise of imagination and agency derived from such creation:

> I believe I am an artist because I truly care about it and I feel connected to it. Whenever I finish an art piece I feel like I can take over the world and get so happy about what I have just created.

CHAPTER 2

A FOCUS ON EMOTION

Springfest Dance Performance

Photograph © by Liza Voll

"My own feelings—not just the character's"

One of the obvious ways in which arts learning differs from other subjects is its deliberate focus on emotion. There is joy in the solution of a math problem and the recognition of its elegance. Students may feel sorry for the cat they are dissecting in biology and outrage at the injustices described in history books. But the expression of joy, compassion, or outrage is not a featured goal of learning in math, biology, or history.

In the arts, however, these emotions are treated directly, and their expression is a frequent learning objective. How do I express joy through the three-dimensional medium of clay? How can I evoke compassion through the gestures of a dance or the emphasis I place on certain musical notes? Can I use lines and shadow to make a sorrowful drawing, an image that might make a viewer sad? How will I make real on stage the outrage of the character I portray?

Expression: How I feel

Ryan is an earnest and articulate 14-year-old who looks you in the eye and speaks with deliberation. A dedicated theater student in an independent secondary school where the arts are valued as academic subjects, Ryan tells me how troubling it was for him when his best friend's father passed away. He couldn't comprehend his friend's isolating sorrow. Ryan offered help, but his friend turned away—as if he would rather be alone with his pain than together with Ryan.

Against this backdrop of distress, Ryan was immediately engaged when his theater teacher assigned a monologue (a frequent activity in high school theater classes) in which Ryan assumed the role of a boy whose parent had died. It enabled him, he told me, to begin to understand the depth of his friend's pain. "Playing the part, getting into someone else's skin the way we do in theater, allowed me to feel from inside out."

Ryan's phrase, "feel from inside out," is a potent descriptor of artistic expression as the representation of authentic emotion. "When I spoke my lines, it was my feeling and not just the character's," Ryan told me. Furthermore, he explained, "I knew I was experiencing at least some of what my friend had been through."

A theater teacher at a technical high school speaks to the point: "I think that empathy is one of the most important lessons that high school aged students can learn . . . and that the theater is uniquely equipped as a forum for learning and practicing it as a skill." He explains:

> I believe that studying the arts, especially theater, is crucial for developing empathy, a skill that is rarely touched on in high schools but seems crucial for healthy development of teenagers and young adults. Studying and participating in drama gives high school students opportunities to recognize emotions and practice different ways of interacting with each other, which are important parts of building empathy. For teenagers who are struggling to fit into a new school culture and negotiate relationships with one another as their bodies and minds mature into adulthood, the ability to recognize emotions in oneself and others is vital for working in society.

Ryan's theater teacher is a veteran director and acting coach. He explains that one of the objectives of the monologue assignment is for "students to learn to tell stories effectively through the eyes of another person." The link in this objective between expression (telling the story effectively) and empathy (through the eyes of another person) highlights the breadth of emotional opportunity in a drama-based encounter with arts learning.

Although Ryan's teacher assigns his monologues randomly, he allows that sometimes "a story hits very close to home," and when that happens, it is easier to find "truth in the text." He shares a related story:

> I had a young African American male student who was very gifted and talented. I was coaching him for his college auditions and as a part of the audition, he was singing a song about his father and how he was a role model to him. Kurt sang the song, but he sang it as if it were a series of notes and melodies. It had no heart or soul to it whatsoever. I sat him down during a coaching session and we discussed how this piece could be a part of his real life. We talked about role models, we talked about family, and we talked about losing someone you love. We made the text accessible and personal to him. We handled the text as a monologue and I helped Kurt create a dialogue between him and God and I asked him to deliver the text as if it were a personal prayer. After doing the monologue several times, I then had him sing it with the same story underscoring the notes. We both cried like babies. He felt safe to express himself and to be personal in front of me and it affected us both.

"Safe to express himself." "Safe" is a frequent descriptor for places reserved for the arts. Like the educational art center in the community, a school's art room, dance, music, or theater studio is often referred to as a safe haven.[1] Art teachers in all domains will expound on the safety of the environments they provide, arenas in which students are able to take the risk involved in expressing emotion from inside out. A 30-year veteran public high school art teacher put it simply: "The art room seems to be the place that students can trust there is peace and understanding . . . from classmates and from the teacher. It is a neutral ground." Another veteran arts teacher and administrator explains:

> I think that high school–aged students, as a group, are reluctant to communicate with adults and sometimes with each other about sensitive issues. Art-making provides a buffer between teens and their "audience" that allows for broaching tough issues, including sexuality, biases of all kinds, depression and suicide, and domestic violence.

Dance teachers will tell you that their studios allow students to feel "safe in the movement so that they don't know or care who is watching them." An independent high school dance teacher explains that this is most challenging because of the vulnerability involved in expressing emotion though your body—especially for students of high school age:

> These kids express emotion through every movement that they make. Their body is their instrument—not the pencil, violin, or voice. And their instrument is the essence of who they are and dance is more vulnerable than any other art form (theater is parallel) because it is really you out there. In theater you play a role. In dance we always address emotion. We work from that emotional context in choreography where we set the steps, but it's never about the steps. It's about the emotion behind the steps.

Music teachers will encourage students to take artistic risks, assuring them that the expression of emotion that is the personal aspect and artistic height of their work is safe from judgments of good or bad. A music teacher told me that one of the most important things he teaches his high school students, along with the "value of hard work," is "the excitement of expression by stretching the student to tell a story through music and their instrument, to go beyond playing it correctly, to connect with the audience, to share the joy of music with the audience."

At a time when the opinions of others are especially important—if not self-determining—it is both risky and fulfilling to share aspects of one's interior self—the emotions evoked by the music one is playing, the sharing of secret sorrow with an audience of strangers. But it is through the expression of our own emotions and the experience of empathy for the feelings of others that personal identity is shaped.

David, an enthusiastic sophomore who is dedicated to drama, told me, "To be honest, I was a complete shit at expressing myself before I was a theater guy, but then I found a release for all that intensity I carried around. I do it because I need to, I have to get all these emotions out there and make them real." A high school theater teacher had similar news: "Doing theater in high school was life-saving for me. It was a form of expression that I would have been incapable of doing any other way at that time of my life."

David explains that it's not just about the emotions you know firsthand, but it's the emotions of others as well: "You can portray any emotion onstage. If you haven't experienced the event, you can make that happen for your character and that is intense and your understanding increases. It's the best way to figure things out." A 9th-grader who prefers the visual arts speaks of himself and other teens in his class: "We can't express the ways we feel with words on a paper as well as we can if we have the option to show how we feel or think by doing it in pictures or drawings or paintings." A senior tells us, "Art silently cries for those who can't."

Through making and finding meaning in art, we discover our capacity to feel and care, to be true to ourselves and responsible for others. This process floods the developmental agenda of the adolescent who predictably tries on different social roles and identities, determining what does and does not fit.[2] In light of such priorities, it is not surprising that the subject and practice of the arts are particularly compelling to students of this age. "Who am I?" "What do I feel?" A 1st-year studio art student—a 9th-grader in a charter high school—describes her experience of personal expression through art:

> One time I drew a girl in pencil that looked [like she] was staring at something blankly, like she didn't have any emotions. It reminded me of a time when I felt like I had no emotions because I was in a tough situation. Art helps me release my feelings on the paper without having to say a word, especially when I don't want to talk. Another time I drew flowers with a gust of wind that looked like ribbons because I felt very calm. For me, art is all about emotions put on a page so you can express yourself in a different, deeper way than words.

Across artistic disciplines, arts teachers and students explain that the high school arts classroom provides a secure and level playing field on which the boundaries of expression and empathy can be explored as means and ends. An experienced acting teacher who has worked with teens beyond school walls explains: "Social roles, whether applied by peers or self-assumed (jock, nerd, cool kid, loser), seem to evaporate when those student artists join forces to accomplish a common goal." Speaking of the ways in which difference is a boon and not an obstacle to artistic expression, he asks, "Where else but the arts does awkwardness have as much merit as physical strength?"

As if she knew the question was out there, a modern dance teacher tells me a particular story of awkwardness becoming strength for one of her high school students:

> A 16-year-old boy took my beginning dance class. He was one of two boys in the class, recently diagnosed with Type I diabetes, and wanted to be a magician when he grew up. This boy was very nice, and very smart, but very shy and not what anyone would describe as coordinated. He had been working in the technical theater department for several years, and had stage-managed for the yearly dance concert the year prior. This boy's awkwardness extended past being all knees and elbows and into his social interactions, as well. While the students at this school were generally very kind, and nobody tortured or bullied this kid (as may have been the case in a rougher school), it was commonly acknowledged that he was a "nerd." This boy came alive in dance class. Whatever the step or combination I gave him, he interpreted it with total abandon ... The boy gained a reputation as an entertainer, and other kids started talking about him as "eccentric," and "cool." He gained confidence, and even poise and grace that leaked into the act he was developing as a magician. This boy decided to step in front of the curtain a lot more often, and is now studying theater in college. If I had to characterize the most substantial life change related to arts learning for this kid, I would have to say that he learned that his particular brand of awkward and offbeat won him friends and a place in perhaps the most treacherous social world we all have to navigate.

Addressing the lessons of expression and empathy, an independent high school freshman tells me that theater "teaches you about other people— things you would never be able to ask." Fourteen-year-old Tina considers the opportunity to play a part as a privilege, a privilege that she calls a "beautiful lic." I am taken by the expression "beautiful lie." Is it original? Did Tina hear the term in recent album titles by Ed Harcourt or 30 Seconds to Mars? The Urban Dictionary defines a beautiful lie as an untruth that makes people feel "good inside even if they know it is not true."[3]

Though surely not intentionally related, that dictionary definition could apply to the activity of role-play, what Tina calls the falseness of pretending to be someone else—"the fun of being mean"—and the truth she finds in the chance "to be more than just me." Tina does not take this opportunity lightly. Key to her success is the willingness to explore her own emotions as access to those of the person she portrays.

Tina recently performed a monologue in the voice of a 30-year-old woman, a woman "more than twice my age"—a woman who was very unhappy in her marriage. But in her preparation, all Tina had was the monologue, no further information about the person she was asked to play. She explains how she addressed this challenge: "I thought about what could be wrong in the marriage and created a problem that would be very upsetting to me: he wasn't paying attention to her."

By having a specific problem in mind (one that she could imagine for herself), Tina was able to engage personally, to invest into her reading what she felt was a convincing absence of self-worth—a feeling of insignificance. "It wasn't hard to play someone older," she explained, "but it was impossible to express how sad she was until I created a problem for her—something real about her unhappy marriage that I could think about as I read the lines."

Tina does not elaborate on her choice of problems and its relative relevance to her own life—beyond something she could relate to directly—but she is clear that what she likes about theater class is the time and opportunity to problem-solve in the fascinating arena of human feelings—to investigate a role and consider the sorts of situations that evoke one emotion or another. "It's not the usual kind of homework," Tina lights up, "but it's hard work and it feels important to my development as a human being."

While a few students in Tina's class see the ability to speak in public as a pragmatic motivation for studying theater, there is general agreement on the draw of personal development and the hard work that Tina describes. "Personal development," "learning about other people," "challenging myself"—for these students, this is where relevance and interest lie.

At an urban high school for the visual and performing arts at which the majority of the student population is minority (African American and Latino) from low-income households, the same elements infuse the packed classroom of Freshman Improvisation. The scenes in rehearsal are being readied for public performance under the guidance of the professional actor and director who teaches the class. The petite young woman whose scene it is is almost completely hidden by an enormous sweatshirt, sunglasses, and a striped woolen skullcap. Slightly bent over under the weight of an overstuffed backpack, she enters the room and looks directly at her cool and confident friend.

"So we disagree," the friend begins, alluding to some offstage debate. "Yeah," the backpacker responds, opening her faded orange wallet and pointing to a photo: "I don't believe in legalizing marijuana." "Who is that dude?" the other young woman inquires first boldly, then quietly: "the one that's been beating on you?" The backpacker nods. A moment of intense mutual consideration is broken when a young man jauntily joins the friend onstage. "Come on, I've got some. Come with me now." With a look of fleeting compassion, the friend goes off with the boy and the backpacker pauses, turns, and walks sadly out the door. Her back seems to have sunk lower; her measured steps embody her sorrow. The applause from students is thunderous. There are tears in the eyes of audience members. I sense they know the identity of the real-life person in the make-believe photo.

In the well-equipped theater studio of a rural independent secondary school or the spare industrial classroom setting of an urban high school, the scene is the same. Adolescents whose problems may be minimized or feared by the general population find shape and audience for their personal pain. These students carry their concerns into every classroom, and attentive teachers of any subject are aware and compassionate.

What a student is enduring outside of class may affect or interrupt her performance in a non-arts subject. But singularly in the arts classroom, what students are experiencing in their lived lives—their personal and often most difficult challenges—are at the center of the action: the means, content, and objective of learning. And it is no small issue that the focus on emotion in these high school arts classes is not an artificial activity; it is just what is featured at the highest levels of professional arts learning.

Empathy: How Others Feel

I am crowded into the auditors' rows in the Thursday night master class of Los Angeles' famed acting coach and teacher Ivana Chubbuck, author of the celebrated book *The Power of the Actor*[4] and mentor to well-known film actors such as Halle Berry and Brad Pitt. I can hear Chubbuck's velvety voice (she has a microphone), but I cannot see her. She faces the actors on the stage, and while I can appreciate the graceful arch of her directing hand, her attention is completely focused on their performance. "So have you had a friend who loves a girl and you know he'll spend less time with you if he spends more time with her?" The actor is nodding. "Speak to that friend."

I am reminded by this encounter among working artists of the work of Urban Improv in Boston,[5] an interactive program in which actors come into the classroom and help students improvise and problem-solve around challenges they are actually facing in their lives. The issues are daunting: violence prevention, conflict resolution, decision-making—keeping each other safe. "Let's play the scene again," a professional actor will say to an impromptu cast of high school students, "but this time, let's try an alternative ending." The student playing a teenager who's been asked to hang out and smoke has an idea. She picks up the phone: "Don't cry, Mom. I'll leave the party early if you need me." With similar methods, drama has been used with success in reducing bullying in schools by assembling the three main actors (the victim, the bully, and the bystander) and using expression and empathy to make sense of the scene.[6]

"What is your objective?" the veteran teacher in the Chubbuck method is asking the professional actor who has prepared a monologue for another class. The teacher is speaking of the goal the actor pursues in the scene or story. The acting student is clear on objective. He wants revenge on the person to whom he is speaking. In preparation, he has employed elements of Chubbuck's technique such as careful script analysis and the heartfelt free-writing of what is called an Emotional Diary.

The student has uncovered a pressing need to inflict pain. His presentation is skillfully done; he has clearly considered each moment. But the teacher wants more. Referring to the person in the actor's life whom the actor uses to generate an organic emotional response, the teacher asks, "Who is your substitution?" The student replies that he is thinking of/speaking to the principal whom he really hated in school. "Is there no one closer to you? Someone closer at whom you are very angry?" The actor thinks hard, racking his brain; he has worked diligently on the monologue, selected a particular individual to whom he is speaking and suddenly he is asked to ditch it all and think of someone else.

"Does he have to be alive?" the student finally asks. "No," the teacher replies. The actor nods solemnly. He has a new person in mind. He begins again and this time the monologue is riveting—there are remnants of the careful pace of his former performance, but his intense emotion now dominates the stage. Classmates and auditors break into applause. The teacher speaks quietly and respectfully, realizing the courage and risk-taking that went into the new version.

His comment is spare but deeply personal: "Well done." And as we leave the studio, the young actor is still on stage, his head between his knees. He is weeping. And everyone is proud and happy for him.

Back at the high school dance studio, I enjoy the view from the edge of this artistic safe space. Young men and women are lined up at the bar. Several of the African American male dancers have their hair in neat cornrows. They wear black tights and white tee shirts and stand with regal elegance. Suddenly a young woman in pink tights and a white-skirted leotard rushes by. She is a tall and graceful junior whose eyes are most obviously filled with tears. I am impressed that she makes no apologies nor seems uncomfortable that others will see her cry. "She's having some major dilemmas," her dance teachers explain; "we just give her space."

"Students cry a lot in class," Alana, a visiting professor of dance, explains as if I should know: "Your body is an instrument." I envision strings pulled tight and feelings close to the surface. She goes on, "Music takes you into this expressive mode." I imagine the well-tuned instrument responding to and reflecting the student dancers' piano accompaniment. And suddenly the young professor cannot stay seated.

Alana leaps to her feet and, with arms and legs extending into sweeping broad movements, demonstrates how students "dance out" their emotions. I am almost overwhelmed by the scale and energy of her movement, the emotional release and expressive detail and the point she makes most visibly: dance speaks an expansive language far different from the words we are using in our seated conversation. The famous Isadora Duncan describes this difference in the statement: "If I could say it, I wouldn't dance it."[7]

For adolescents whose feelings are so close to the surface, literally and metaphorically, the nonverbal language of dance (the arts discipline least taught in schools) may be particularly vibrant and immediate. I observe as a young male dance teacher explains to a studio filled with student athletes and others of various sizes and shapes that Merce Cunningham said that all movement was dance—the impatient jiggle of a foot, the stumble off a riser in the gym. The students seem especially engaged, taken aback and intrigued by this claim, aware that the very way in which each of them was sitting at attention on the floor was particular and expressive, letting others know something of who each of them was and what perhaps they were feeling at that moment.

Pointing to the importance of dance to high school–age students who are embroiled in the throes of change and expectation, the dance professor shares that when she hit puberty the enormous physical engagement and expressive release of dance helped her through all sorts of emotional issues. "It's not always a conscious enterprise," she explained. "A student who goes wild in a hip-hop class, lost in a vigorous dance explosion, may realize after the fact that he is working off his disappointment at not making the football team." A ballet student's poignant gestural interpretation of a piece of music makes onlookers cry, and, perhaps surprised by their response, she realizes that she is mourning the death of her grandmother.

A pair of high school students, disciplined young ladies, attracted to ballet because of the structure and clear objectives that it provides ("I know what I'm striving for"), agreed that "a big aspect of performance is the expression of emotion, engaging with the audience with your eyes or the flick of a hand." Indeed, both of them told me that the personal expression of emotion, like creativity, was the highest achievement of their art form, something that they realized you attain in dance only after you've mastered the techniques.

The word "personal" appears frequently in the vocabulary of teachers of any of the arts. Like the acting teacher who suggested that making it personal —making it about the student's real life—made the difference for his theater student's performance, teachers in other art forms point to the personal nature of artistic expression as a gateway to student learning.

Gary, a veteran high school arts teacher who now teaches at the college level, tells me that when painting and drawing students come to understand "the making and the materials as personal symbol systems," they begin to comprehend how much of themselves they can put into or express through their work. As his visual arts students' skills increase, they discover that expression in art relies on the manipulation of symbols, the student's unique personal mark on form or out of line: "fingers in clay or the movement of that pencil can communicate meanings that are so different."

Gary suspects that in many non-arts classes, high school students feel that it's all about memorizing information in which they don't play a part. Students' ideas can't change the content they've been asked to learn. But in their arts classes, they find that their ideas and feelings make a big difference, and that self-expression provides both content and purpose to their learning. A high school senior who takes electives in oil painting and drawing says of her artwork, "It doesn't come from an outside source. It comes from within the individual and it is more about you than about conforming."

"It's an empowering realization" a visual arts teacher and department head describes the time when high school students master the basic technical skills ("which everyone can learn just as they can learn to write or do math") and find opportunities "to express themselves in the means that works best for them." A high school gallery full of foundational and advanced two- and three-dimensional visual arts students' work makes the point.

Eighteen green hammers hung carefully in a row ask the viewer to hear the story they tell even as the tiny differences in the angles at which they hang are oddly moving, begging the viewer to find variety and stillness in apparent similarity and repetition. Large black-and-white photos—more painterly than precise—reflect students' directed quest to see light rather than objects and speak to the emotive quality of imprecision. Expressive drawings of skulls herald the first step in a portraiture project, while painted landscapes and self-portraits demonstrate students' developing skills at constructing representational images and imbuing them with emotive power.

The work (tangible products) by these high school artists is presented with the same respect and attention as the work of professionals, and that treatment is both honoring and appropriate. In this light, the viewer encounters the sensitivity of vision and quest for self-expression of these young artists as well as the place they and their work strive for and deserve in the cultural enclaves of the adult world.

A dynamic Ivy League–bound senior who is dedicated to her painting and drawing explains the pride she had in having her work in the gallery show and seeing others study and compliment it. In a school in which sports seem to be the dominant mode, Rachel tells me of the group of young women who spent time studying her self-portrait and finally said to her with newfound admiration, "Oh, so that's why you're not playing lacrosse." Rachel shares that last year she had a "mental breakdown: one thing after another went wrong" and she almost dropped out of school. What saved her was the peaceful refuge she found in the art studio, the opportunity to listen to her iPod and "submerge" herself in her portrait painting.

I am reminded by Rachel's story of a painting that hangs in my living room. It's a childlike scratch-out portrait (the image is scratched with a tool out of poster paint layered over wax crayon) of a tense-looking woman, hands curled to her heart, holding a bent flower. Somewhat older than Rachel when I created the image, I was extremely anxious and finished the work with surprising intensity and speed. When it was done, I was astonished to see that I was relieved of the emotion that had consumed me. It had found its place in the portrait that I created, and I can see it there still.

A public high school fine arts instructor describes the power of students' emotional investment in the arts and the notion of a safe space as enduring beyond one's life at school:

> I was the director of the school play and one of my students who was particularly weak in reading was auditioning. He was so motivated with regard to getting the part that he not only memorized his part, but

those of the other characters in the play. Years later he returned to visit me, and shared that he had been in and out of correctional schools and facilities since he graduated but his opportunity to be center stage in that show is what kept him from taking his life on several occasions. Remembering the audience's response to his performance literally had saved his life.

Another theater teacher describes a similar situation regarding a young man we can call Robert, a student at a high school for the emotionally disturbed where the teacher had led a residency:

> Like many of his fellow students, Robert was a foster child who was raised in a violent home, and the culture of the school was often threatening and dangerous. I hoped that the workshops I offered, which focused on improvisation and an adaptation of *The Old Man and the Sea,* could allow the students a new opportunity to work cooperatively and practice respect and empathy. In that sense, the residency seemed successful for nearly everyone involved, but this one young man was particularly moved. He confided that he always wanted to learn more about performing, but constant name-calling and taunting from his peers at school prohibited him from pursuing it. The chance to participate in a group of students, all working on creating a performance, gave him the support he needed to excel. Moreover, when he was distinguished as a talented actor—when he made his peers laugh with him—he gained the confidence to make more friendships in school and the emotional strength to push on in school . . . and I believe that his experience directly improved his academic learning as well as his social and emotional development.

We have not done and clearly cannot do reliable quantitative studies of the impact of self-expression through the arts on social and emotional development or the adolescent's developing sense of self-worth. But through the resonant stories of teachers and students, we recognize the worth of these experiences—perhaps especially to those students who eschew classes that more reasonably invite measurement. The importance of self-expression and self-esteem is cited everywhere in the stories and voices of arts students and teachers at the high school level. But just as these individuals celebrate the arts for the opportunity they provide to express, release, recognize, and own emotions, others worry that the arts "stir things up." The arts are perhaps rightly charged with bringing messy feelings to the fore in classrooms that are more tidily based around content learning and performance on standardized tests.

An 11th-grader in a public high school makes the point, "I'm eager to come to art class because I love art and I'm liberated here. I'm free to express anything I'm feeling. No other class offers me that." A 12th-grade graffiti writer says that for him, the most important thing about art-making and learning is quite simply "freedom of expression."

The opportunities that arts learning provides for these adolescents are essential. In the study of young adults who had dropped out of high school, only 41% said that they felt there was someone in the school whom they could go to with their personal issues.[8] As might so many of the great teachers in all and any subjects, the keepers of the safe haven that is the arts classroom would have served these former students well.

A fledgling visual arts teacher in a science-based public high school experienced the power of the safe haven when the arena he had created for the safe expression of the personal was tested by a 10th-grader:

> I had a student recently "come out" to me while working on a drawing of two girls making out. She had spent the entire class hiding her drawing under her shirtsleeves and notebooks, until finally another student said, "He isn't going to care! Just say it!" and this student, meekly asked if I would allow her to continue that drawing. I was so stunned I just asked, "Uhhh, why would you not be able to?" completely dumbfounded. And she pointed out the two figures were female . . . . and paused . . . "Again," I said, "I'm really not sure why you're asking this question. It's two people making out. They're kissing. It's a beautiful moment. So you want to know what I think? You need to punch up your shading around the jawlines if you want more drama. Those shadows should be directing the viewer's eyes to the areas of the picture YOU want them to go. Does that answer your question?" And with a big toothy grin, she just said, "Yes."

Nourishing the Soul

Adolescents and their powerful emotions and self-discoveries are in sync with the anti-standardization of the arts. Young people are drawn to the idiosyncratic expression and human development that the arts afford. The focus on emotion in the arts—whether in the soulful interpretation of a theatrical monologue, the vibrant motion of a modern dance, or the powerful construction of a drawing or sculpture—results in two learning outcomes that are of great interest and importance to high school–age students: 1) expression, the opportunity to give shape to one's own feelings and 2) empathy, the discovery of others' similar or different emotions as embodied in works of art.

Advocates who struggle with finding a more secure place for the arts in mainstream education, let alone a central spot in the high school curriculum, will protest, "Try convincing a school board that expression and empathy are worthy learning goals. You'll be laughed out of the room. We've done a lot to convince administrators that the arts are comprised of serious intellectual (i.e., non-emotional) endeavors, even including a view of the construction of emotion out of artistic symbols as a cognitive activity—a triumph of head and not an indulgence of heart."[9]

These tired objections must not be tolerated. When it comes to the effectiveness of high school education, we are at a time of crisis and in need of more repair than can emerge from a semantic debate. When high schools are about what students need and want to know, students will try harder to show up and stay in school. The developmental portrait of the high school student must govern our decisions of what we offer during the school day.

Adolescence is a time at which intense emotions run high. High school–age students are characterized as impetuous and dramatic on the one hand, capable of sophisticated abstract thinking on the other. They are able to assume roles with authenticity, produce and decipher metaphors, and vest and find emotional content in works of art. They rightly appreciate respectful preprofessional rapport, value the safe havens that the arts create, and seize the attendant opportunities for shaping and expressing identity and vision.

Keenly aware of the power and content of emotion, high school students are appropriately preoccupied with their personal growth. The arts are uniquely situated to provide the tools for development and the opportunity for students to experience their individual inscription on whatever artistic symbols they employ. These aspects of arts learning have meaning for students of all ages, but adolescents are particularly drawn to the brave focus on expressing and discovering feelings that the arts invite. A theater teacher explains:

> Acting, studying, and critiquing scenes gives students a chance to
> experience and view different emotions and see the results of different

actions that result. Playwriting gives students a chance to invent conflicts for characters and explore the effects of different approaches to solve or circumvent them.

A 16-year-old bilingual public high school student who experienced a 7-week immersion program in the arts put it succinctly:

> The arts in, really in every different form of the arts, be it painting or sculpting or acting or, you know, creating music, anything I think, it's a completely different type of learning. It, you know, nourishes your soul, and it just allows you a freedom that you don't get in the normal classroom and school a lot of times. . . . I know that people need to be able to explore themselves, express themselves, and create, and it's not something that you're always able to do in just the normal context of the classroom.

CHAPTER 3

Ambiguity

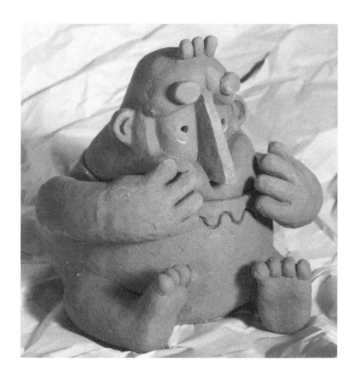

Ceramic "Lazlo"

Artist, David Wang (Class of 2010)

Photograph by Dani Coleman

"Where meaning is up for grabs"

There is little dispute that standardized tests most accurately measure right or wrong answers. But what about answers that fall in between? If we multiply 15 times 100, for example, we are right when we say the result is 1,500 and wrong when we say the answer is 15,000. However, if we are asked if 1,499 is a righter wrong answer than 15,000, things get complicated. You may argue that 1,499 is only one integer away from 1,500 and therefore closest to right. But knowing that the student who came up with 15,000 was rightly calculating by adding zeros to 15, I might argue that she was just as close to right—only 1 point away. Below the crystal-clear surface of right or wrong answers, we can easily find murky water. And while surface-diving may help to understand our students' reasoning, when we are looking for a standardized numerical score, right or wrong tells the whole story.

Right or wrong tells the whole story with all kinds of factual information such as signings of historical documents and lengths of wars (history), classifications of vertebrate versus invertebrate (science), or sums in addition (math). And when presenting the sort of well-defined information that can ultimately be tested for, the objective is to be as distinct and precise as possible. Vertebrates have backbones. Invertebrates do not. Clear-cut nonnegotiable meaning is the stuff of right answers. Most high school students have traveled this territory for over a decade, since their very first worksheets where they got a check for coloring in orange when the word under the circle was "orange" and an "Excellent" on the top of the page when they made no mistakes. This crisp-edged and familiar terrain marks another important way in which the contents of arts learning differs from that of other subjects.

Interpretation: My Perspective Matters

The meaning of a work of art is always negotiable. It is invariably blurry and debatable, open to as many understandings as makers and perceivers of the work can reasonably defend. "This painting is so sad," a teenager in an art museum might say looking at a painting filled with heavy downward lines. "Why do you say that?" another might ask. "Well, it feels gloomy and sorrowful, all that sinking weight." But the other student may counter, "Wow, I find the weight comforting, strong—grounded. And the colors the artists uses—all those earthy tones—speak to me of solidarity and strength."

Both students have interpreted what they see. They have taken the elements presented in the work and put them together in ways that makes sense to them. Furthermore, they have justified their analyses—explained their different interpretations of sadness versus strength (two meanings that are in any case not mutually exclusive). From listening to each other's perspectives, both of them may have found something new within the work—or a new way of looking at the work. "Yes, but which one is right?" "Neither and both."

"Which one is righter?" A third viewer may find more evidence for the claims of one teen over the other. Or she may want to share that she read somewhere that the artist was exploring nihilism in this work. This contribution sparks a lively back-and-forth. But none of this active learning, challenging discourse, and thoughtful reflection can be reduced to right or wrong. All of it is beyond the scope of standardized measurement. And all of it is important to learn.

High school–age students, navigating the transition to the complex, often-contradictory world of adulthood, need to be able to acknowledge and consider multiple perspectives. Furthermore, they need to understand and value their central role in their own learning—their own ability to make and find meaning that seems "right" (if only for a while) to them.

In the usually austere environment of the art museum, resident experts most often lecture to visitors, advising them to consider aspects of the work that they might never have considered on their own. While the museum is a treasure trove of valuable information, the heart of the experience lies in viewers' individual and group encounters with the timeless tangible products of artistry that line the walls.[1]

An art museum educator who focuses on inquiry-based learning (asking and listening to questions) in the art museum told me that:

> Students are often amazed to realize that they are the ones—both individually and collectively—who create meaning in the museum around the works of art. (I think that teachers learn a ton from this experience as well—seeing that the students are creating the meaning and that the meaning is not defined by art historians and curators.)

The arts take us beyond the apparently sharp-edged landscape of factual information to the blurry haze of negotiated meaning-making: the construction of meaning on the part of the creator of the work and the construction of meaning on the part of the beholder, reader, or listener. Somewhere in between the making and the perceiving, meaning is found. And repeated experiences with the work often awaken additional and/or new understandings.

On account of this constructive exchange, an encounter with a work of art is often likened to a conversation between artist and viewer. "What questions does this painting ask you?" "What questions do you wish to ask it?" "What questions does this painting ask you a year later?" Because of the layers of meaning in a work of art, the conversation continues and takes new hues and depth from one to another meaning-maker or the same meaning-maker over time.

High school students (especially those who have had opportunities in arts learning) are positioned not only to consider the aesthetic elements or story line of a work of art, but also to consider the challenges that face an artist creating a work. For example, younger children are expected to respond to the question, "How do you think the artist who made this work might have felt?" by thinking that a sad painting or song is the work of a sorrowful artist. But adolescents can apprehend the conscious purposefulness of artistry—the idea that an artist might explore sorrow (whether she was sad or not) or exuberance (even on a bad day) through the available or selected artistic medium.[2]

This maturity enables adolescents to address questions like, "What problems was the artist posing for himself?" as he addressed the work of making a painting, writing a play, choreographing a dance, or composing a musical composition. "What associations do you have with what you see or read or hear?" "What ideas do you find expressed in this work?" "Where do you find the work's value?" "Does the work interest you? Why or why not?" Questions like these invite a range of considerations and multiple (though interestingly similar and different) personally relevant reflections.

It is important to note the obvious: that arts education has its share of factual information. This has been the mantle of many advocates challenged by the assertion that the only subjects worth studying are those in which learning can be measured on standardized tests. "Hey, the arts have facts, too. Their histories are replete with dates, identifiable styles, births and deaths of famous artists, and changing artistic movements. What about art history slide shows where students identify (rightly or wrongly) the creator of the work being shown?"

We need to learn (and our learning can be tested) about the color wheel, the tones indicated by various notes on a page of music, the names of Shakespeare's various plays, and the transformative performances in the history of modern dance. But other advocates will argue that these informational points of reference are either contextual or technical. They inform but do not describe what's most significant about the arts: the act of making and the achievement of expression (as discussed earlier)—the exploration of possibility and challenge that connects human beings across circumstance and time.

Talking with teachers of a range of subjects, I offered this perspective, arguing that the questions that were most important in art education were those that did not have right or wrong answers. To everyone's surprise, the head of the local high school's math department declared with certainty, "Same thing with math." She explained that in math and she thought in science as well the facts and procedures that we study (and can test for) are merely stepping-stones toward the exciting challenges of the field.

It may be said for all fields that factual information is no more than fodder for the real questions that drive our work, those questions to which we do not have answers or to which there is not just one answer. But this broad-based implicit lesson is explicitly available in the study of the arts, where what obviously matters is not the still end states of right or wrong but the active process of putting things together; using information, tools, and skills—applying them to the discovery and pursuit of further exploration. It is the quest—the navigation of blurry boundaries between what we see and know, what we imagine and consider, what is presented and what is meant. The deliberate ambiguity of works of art challenges the learner to stretch beyond the given and actively critique possible understandings.

In arts education, we learn that multiple possibilities enrich the direction of each stroke of the painter's brush, the shape of each gesture of the dancer, the selection of each word of the poem. From the study of the ambiguity of art, then, students are introduced to two important learning outcomes: 1) interpretation: the decoding of meaning through which I realize that my perspective, which may vary from others' and change over time, matters; and 2) respect: the understanding that others' perspectives (their meaning-finding and -making) do the same and are always worthy of my regard.

In interpreting a work of art, we learn to learn from one another and to enlarge our vision through what each other sees, rather than to compare which of us has the most and truest information. A 10th-grade arts student answers my question of what is the most important thing that the arts have taught him:

> I guess to keep an open mind is the most important thing anyone
> can learn. This fact is conveyed in a bunch of art classes. Without an
> open mind you won't get far and if you are going to say, "Uh, that is
> interesting" instead of shirking off to the side, you'll be open to taking in

all of the ideas that present themselves. [It's] the opposite of judgmental or close-minded where everything is shut down immediately.

Teenagers today are mass consumers of electronic media, sharing their lives on social networks, keeping in touch through text and voice messaging, and launching their personal presentations in sprawling venues like YouTube. These young people have acquired, through their technical consumption, vocabularies and skills beyond those of many of us trying to teach them. Still, they need to be reminded that the representations in the media are there for interpretation—not uncritical acceptance. As one arts teacher pointed out, "High school students are saturated by visual media through Facebook and Twitter, but that doesn't mean they're thinking deeply about it."

Adolescents are extensively portrayed and largely stereotyped throughout what is known as our visual culture: the visual media that surround us including fine art, the images in comic books, movies, electronic games, and iconic advertising symbols for various products. The rapper with the baggy pants and skateboard; the preppy with the plaid headband and ballet flats; the school jock with the short blond hair; everyone with some version of a piercing or tattoo and all of them resisting or relishing alcohol and drugs. Hovering around the edges are nerds (often the hidden heroes) with thick eyeglasses or artistic types dressed in black, sporting edgy if not scary hooded sweatshirts.

The media has always loved to parody the extremes of adolescence—the deeply felt emotions, the storming sexuality, the threat of real mental illness or metaphoric vampire attack, the struggle for acceptance across economic and social lines. The 350 years between Shakespeare's star-crossed teenage lovers and their counterparts in the Broadway show and movie *West Side Story* did not dilute the power of the story.[3] The replacement of warring families with enemy gangs served only to highlight the central theme of the adolescent's struggle to make his or her own decisions and overcome flawed reality with true love.

More recently, the movie *Easy A* (2010) extended Nathaniel Hawthorne's 19th-century exploration of illicit love (*The Scarlet Letter*) into a modern-day California high school.[4] The community is turned upside-down by a witty teenage heroine who manipulates the challenges of sexual identity and social acceptance and transcends the land mines of prejudice and rejection. While playfully addressed, these are serious concepts with which real-world high school students struggle as they fashion the identities that will take them into and through the adult world.

Consider media representations of minority teens (African Americans, Latinos, and Native Americans)—those identified in recent studies as three times more likely than their Caucasian classmates to drop out of high school.

While moving portrayals such as the movies *Boyz n the Hood*[5] and *Precious*[6] seriously address the odds for survival (let alone graduation from high school) that face many teens, there is always the risk of enforcing rather than debunking stereotypes. High school students need to have the confidence and skills to make active meaning of these and the myriad of other images that flood the Internet, video games, music videos, and social networks. This is certainly true for gay, lesbian, transgender, and queer youth, who have been identified as most vulnerable in their teens for suicidal ideation and attempts.[7]

While sensitive portrayals can be found throughout the media, and the Internet has provided inspiring interventions,[8] negative representations and commentary abound and can be especially harmful. It is imperative that all our young people have the ability to apply critical interpretive skills. Essential as well to the media meaning-making that young people must do is the respect (for their own and others' perspectives) that is generated from individual and collective interpretation.

Respect: Others' Perspectives Matter

Adolescents must learn to realize that the range of media depictions is merely fodder for the development of their own worldview, not a right answer or an accurate definition into which they must buy. High school students need the skills to question and explore and the confidence to pursue the quest. A graduating senior put it quite simply: "The most important thing I have learned in my art classes is that everyone has a voice." A high school dance teacher explained: "The most important thing I share with my students is respect for who they are."

In recent years, arts educators have assumed what is called a visual culture approach[9] in which teachers conscientiously cultivate skills of interpretation with the focused objective that students become critical manipulators and consumers of the visual image in its many commercial and noncommercial iterations. Firsthand experience with making social statements out of various arts media and interpreting others' representations are essential educational encounters for the 21st-century high school student. In a world in which the media has both facilitated the activity of bullying and raised relevant social consciousness, students need interpretive skills with which to deconstruct and critique our preoccupation with violence.

Respect for others' perspectives motivates front-row students whose hands are always raised to attend to and learn from the boy in the back of the room who may struggle with his courses. His deep insight into a particular poem or image may surprise and inform the other students' take on it all. A variation of Maxine Greene's "Awakeness" includes awakeness to others' perspectives. But others' perspectives will only be heard if the questions posed in class are open-ended and invite multiple responses. "That everyone has a voice."

Considering the movies mentioned above, open-ended questions go beyond closed facts like the names of actors in the cast or the details of plots. They introduce questions of filmmaker intention, relative resonance for students of one character or action over another, or overall effectiveness of the aesthetic work. These are questions that invite multiple and equally valid points of view. Students in a visual culture class might be asked to consider the extent to which media-generated images of youth have an influence on young people's development of self-image. Responses to questions like these inform and expand the understandings of the student offering the perspective and for others who are developing their own. In this mode, students are encouraged to value their own questions and to find on their own the information they need to propel their self-selected pathways of learning.

High school students might decide or be asked to explore their personal inquiries through their own artistic creations. They might consider directly whether and how works of art inspire this sort of interpretation and inquiry. The change in view toward information as a tool, not as an end in itself, calls for a different balance in the classroom. As one high school art teacher explained it: "My approach to teaching teenagers is largely student-based. I like to offer students information as a resource and let them create and lead their own learning." A dance teacher explained how she offered information as a tool for her students:

My approach, and that of the entire department, is student-centered. We introduce students to a wide range of dance genres, choreographers, and productions, and give them the technical tools to express themselves through dance. We then encourage students to reflect on what masterworks or styles resonate with them, and to experiment with interpreting their own emotions and ideas through movement. This type of approach based on positive regard and respect for teens' creative and intellectual contributions provides a strong foundation for an open and productive relationship between the students and instructors.

A visual arts student explained how personal direction and discovery played out for her in her art classes:

> In an upper-level art class, it's more focused on creating a creative
> relationship in which you can formulate ideas together and take
> guidance from the teacher in the direction you have personally
> chosen. There's more freedom to choose your own path or style, make
> philosophical or personal discoveries yourself. Art class prepares a
> student for intellectual adventure, a concept that can be applied to any
> subject in school.

It is true at every developmental stage, and poignantly true at the transitional stage of adolescence, that difference is the governing reality. Students are wrestling with the lonely work of sorting themselves out from the rest even as they long to belong to and/or identify with one group or another. Visiting at an arts high school recently, I was taking in the expected unstated dress code of all black with some variation of wildly colored hair. One of the students read my mind and smiled at me: "Yup. We're all different in the same way."

At my 20th high school reunion of a cliquey cookie-cutter girls' school, alumnae were deciding which of the students in our class had been undeniably "in." I ventured to name the absolutely most popular Susan, and she was horrified at the possibility. "Oh no, I never felt I fit in." And so it went around the room. Who would have known that the outside that all of us were feeling in my high school class was the in—the governing reality for us all? The expectation for sameness that some of us thought others had reached was unrealized. Difference was the given, sameness the illusion.

When curriculum includes (seriously includes) opportunities for students to find mutual respect in their various self-presentations and understandings, the dominance of black/white, right/wrong, or in/out can be overturned with an expectation for gray; the discovery that a good question is more important than any answer; and the realization that we are all together in figuring it out. The teacher's attitude is clearly what sets the stage for this sort of mutual respect and regard for learning from others. A veteran (40 years) visual arts teacher described the process:

> In art classes students are given problems to solve and criteria
> (boundaries) within which to create a possible solution. They are forced
> to take chances, make decisions, and deal with ambiguity. This art-making
> model of problem solution is much more like real-world performance

than most of what goes on in schooling. In addition, it allows room for many diverse, successful solutions to the same problem. Answers (solutions) may be similar, but are never identical and the outlier ideas are often the most exceptional and worthy of the greatest reward (A+).

Further, he tells me how his students, whom he treats "as I would treat any adult because that is how they see themselves . . . I never belittle or talk down to them," respond to the ambiguity he builds into the problems he poses:

They often tell me that they feel a sense of accomplishment when they have worked their way past the initial confusion, created their own solution, and realized there was no "right" answer. Unfortunately, I often find that students with the highest GPAs, those who have had the most academic success, become the most frustrated as they search in vain for that "right" answer.

At a high-powered independent boarding school, replete with high GPAs, the arts department chair expressed a similar sentiment: "I believe that at a school like [this], the arts are of an even greater value—with so many students who know how to find the 'right' answer, the open-endedness and ambiguity and creativity of the arts becomes of paramount importance as students search for their own, personal answers." In light of the popular sentiment that the arts should be reserved for those with particular talent or those students unable to achieve in other academic areas, these comments about high achievers are particularly salient.

All our students need encounters with, and those who have access celebrate, ambiguity and its attendant skills of interpretation and attitudes of respect. A 9th-grader in an urban high school told me what he values most about his arts classes: "The most important thing I have learned is seeing things from different perspectives and being able to analyze things with a deeper meaning, or on a higher level. The artwork really makes you think." Another 9th-grader, this one in a charter school, distinguished her arts classes from the others. Beginning with the stress factor that fills so many student comments, she explained:

Art class isn't stress-inducing. When you walk in the room you immediately feel respect and interest in your opinion and art. The teachers are genuinely interested in the philosophy of your art—or lack thereof.

This interest on the part of teachers in what students think is a key ingredient in the draw of the arts classrooms. Teachers of the arts repeatedly refer
to their students as fellow artists—collaborators in learning—and they look
forward to "what they will teach me" each day. A school headmaster agreed
that the sense of respect (for themselves as well as for others) that students feel
and gain from making sense in and of the arts makes all the difference:

> I think that one of the things that saves lives is kids coming to see that
> people are interested in them and that they have something of interest to
> offer the world. Kids who are negatively identified become so suspicious,
> not daring to believe that they have something good in them, and the
> arts provide a remarkable opportunity for them to learn that they have
> something to offer.

The headmaster's observation would seem to address one of the largest
concerns that adult students who'd left high school reported: "If only they'd
known who I was . . ." Making sense of art together, considering one another's
points of view, cultivates respect not only between teachers and students,
students and other students, but between students and themselves.

The headmaster told me a story about an accomplished student from
China who was a "brilliant physics student" and went on to thrive at an Ivy
League college but came back to tell this compassionate administrator that
his best experiences had been in high school, studying the piano, performing
in concerts. His work in the arts at the headmaster's school, this young man
told him, had made all the difference: "It made me seem interesting to myself."

A high school music teacher told me of a student who was now "an investment banker in some big city." The teacher was surprised to receive a letter
from him that said in part:

> Looking at what I have done—and do now—since graduating . . . may, at
> the surface, not appear relevant to my time playing the clarinet, but what
> I learned from you—your care as a teacher and devotion to music—
> greatly influences my actions and decisions and is a key part of who I
> have become. For that, I am deeply grateful.

Whether the subject at hand is a painting, musical performance, or media
image created by others, interpretation and respect are powerful agents in the
development of personal thought and identity. Adults who have dropped out
of school decry what they experienced as low expectation on others' part and a

lack of involvement in learning on their own. Low expectations are as deficient of respect as active interpretation exudes it.

Many Possible Answers

When students are asking the questions or being asked questions that have many possible answers, when they can experience the power of obtaining information that is interesting to them and putting it to work to generate new questions, there is a sense of ownership of learning that is exciting and relevant. When I determine what and how I learn (even if it is just on my own time in the art room where I decide what product I will make next or what sense I make of others' works of art), I feel empowered and engaged. Perhaps most important, the recognition of difference and validity, even among one's own changing understandings, demands respect. Respect is required for others' perspectives and interpretations as well as one's own.

When the subject matter is ambiguous (thickly layered with potential meaning), as the arts conspicuously and intentionally are, the learning outcomes of interpretation and respect can bolster students who may not be finding a sense of their own control over learning in other subjects. The ability to control one's own production of multiple meanings and to take charge of one's own investigation of meaning in the work of others is exciting, perhaps even an extension of what Dollie McLean has called "the kind of high we want our kids to be feeling every day." A senior whose first language was Spanish explained:

> If you can get a lot of people involved in one thing, they all have different opinions, they can all share different experiences, and stuff you can learn from everybody else . . . It's not just going to school, learn, and get grades and tests. It's not just that. There's a lot more stuff to do. You're dealing with other people. You're trying to make something happen.

CHAPTER 4

PROCESS ORIENTATION

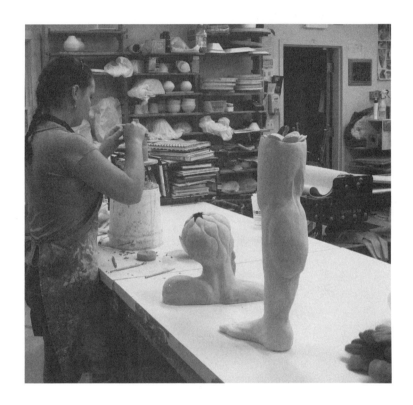

Advanced Placement Ceramics

Photograph by Lloyd Hamovit

"How making a mistake is an opportunity"

On the top floor of the arts building at a suburban independent high school, a sprawling visual arts studio is overflowing with natural light, displays of student works, works in progress, and a densely decorated floor adorned with images and words, a mélange of color crossing the lines between studio paint drippings, artistic sketches, and gorgeous graffiti. Hanging from the ceiling a large white papier-mâché bird seems to gesture and float. Lovely "first-try" stained glass constructions filter the light through one of the many windows that illuminate the expansive space.

A library of art books and magazines awaits student perusal and, happily, shows the wear of real attention. This is a big empty space available for student use at any time to fulfill an arts homework assignment, to work on an individual project, or to produce entries for a student portfolio for a college application. "It can be lonely," a teacher tells me, "for a dedicated arts student working up here on her own." Lonely, perhaps. But so few high school students have the opportunity to work in such inspiring surroundings.

Inquiry: What Next?

On the second level of the same arts building, a veteran high school arts teacher is demonstrating the basics of ceramics to a group of beginning students. The ceramics studio is large and multichambered, with a separate room for firing and glazing. The 12 young male students come from an assortment of grade levels, from 10th to postgraduate. I am astonished to see that a dress code applies even in the art studio. They wear dress shirts, Shetland sweaters (in winter this is permissible in lieu of a sports coat), ties—all marginally protected by studio aprons. I am to discover that the boys are free to dress down for their arts classes, but a shortage of time (time is the school "nemesis") makes it hard for them to change between classes.

Amidst large buckets of clay, well-used worktables, carefully sorted tools, and enough potting wheels for all the students, Ms. Meadow is extremely well organized. She has carefully prepared tangible examples of the different stages of the process that she demonstrates. She sits at her wheel gracefully balancing a clear verbal explanation of her action and an impressive show of coordinated movement: hand and tool around the clay, steady foot on the wheel. She is showing how air bubbles need to be removed, how a certain thickness must be maintained, how to attend to a center, when all at once her tone changes from practical to dreamy and she reminds the students that this is about "touch." "Close your eyes," she offers as a way to fully encounter the process. As she demonstrates her magic in a kind of dramatic reverie (eyes closed, head pointed to the sky), the students look at one another incredulously. I think I hear someone mumble, "No way." Ms. Meadow explains that students must center themselves, leave their anger outside the door, and think of their best friends or whatever else takes their minds to a good place from which they can engage fully in this work.

The students watch their teacher carefully, intent on learning the process and eager to try what she has made look so easy. They are sent off to prepare blocks of clay for their wheels, cautioned that they had best prepare four blocks so that an extra will be available when a first try fails. They are too excited. Each student prepares one wedge of clay and heads swiftly for his wheel. Ms. Meadow urges her students to throw their clay on the wheel with "attitude," and some of them get right to it. Others are reticent; one young man is remarkably cautious: his piece of clay is small, his movements constrained. Putting herself in the latter category, Ms. Meadow explains that there are always some ceramicists who "get it" right away, but others must try the process several times before they are satisfied with their work.

One young man epitomizes the first category, turning out a pot with the ease of an expert. He is clearly pleased by the admiration of the students around him, surprised and delighted by the facility he shows. "Finally something I'm good at," he declares with emphasis. Another young man seems initially disgusted. He is neatly dressed and distressed at messing up his clothes. "Shit," he mumbles under his breath when he first touches the clay. He quickly rises and goes to the sink to wash his hands. This happens twice. I think to myself that he is unlikely to enjoy or to get very far in ceramics, but when I look back at him again, his wheel is spinning at what seems to be 60 miles an hour.

The initially reticent student is apparently unaware that the other students are working at a different, more controlled speed. He appears to be in what the psychologist Csikszentmihalyi has called a state of "flow"—so fully engaged in his own artistic process that he is unaware of what is going on around him.[1] His wheel is spinning, his clay is getting wetter and wetter, he is moment-to-moment literally becoming one with the medium. While other students are gingerly rinsing their fingers in the plastic buckets of water in front of them, this young man is dipping in his whole hand, a large sponge he has taken from the sink, both his hands. And while other students are cleaning the wheel around their pots, his is mounting with clay; his fingers are thickly coated.

I fear for him as Ms. Meadow makes her rounds, gently offering suggestions for improvement of each individual student's work, but she attends to this messy student with the same respect. "It's getting too wet; you need to start again . . . " she advises kindly, and she moves on to the next burgeoning ceramicist. The head of the school's art department has used the term "talented" to describe those students whose gifts and attitudes make them candidates for further study in the arts. I am wondering which of these students displays talent: the careful achiever with the near-perfect pot, or the young man whose excitement about the process has erased what seemed a genuine interest in staying tidy?

All the students seem to enjoy their work. Ms. Meadow regrets they must end so early. She offers to do their cleanup for them. She doesn't have another class right after. But for the most part, they clean up themselves, washing their tools, putting them in the appropriate sorted containers. Ms. Meadow assures them that the muddied water in their plastic pots will miraculously get their hands quite clean, and it turns out that she is right.

The story of the tidy young man lost in his messy process offers an apt example of what the arts particularly offer to students: deep involvement in the doing—a process orientation. It is not just in the finished pots that the students find and display their learning; it is in the reverential process, the careful and inspired making that their teacher has demonstrated with love and skill. "How will I achieve that texture in the pot?" "Look, I'm doing well—finally, something I excel at."

The vivid, engaging process orientation of arts learning invites yet another kind of inquiry, questions that fuel the process of learning rather than the product of a response. Ralph, a Midwestern visual arts teacher with lots of experience, tells me that the most important thing his students learn is "Inquiry—thinking deeply about things, realizing there is not one way to do it. We go through multiple methods as we experience inquiry in making, thinking through materials in new fashions."

In making a work of sculpture or rehearsing a dance or soliloquy, we experience questions of self-assessment such as, "What do I want or need to know to move forward?" Ralph says we need to "talk through with each of these students why they are making decisions—meet with them in small groups—consider what the sculpture is saying and what has been achieved with the clay and is that in line with what your desires and goals were for this piece. Would you change something? Go do it."

The process orientation of arts learning invites purposeful reflection: "How am I doing?" "How do I need to adjust my process to affect a differ-

ent tone or shape in the product that I am creating?" Against such an honest self-reflective backdrop, grades or quantitative scores seem wrong-headed.
Dr. Lissa Soep is the research director and senior producer at Youth Radio, a
well-known organization that educates young people (80% of whom are low
income and/or youth of color) about the media and features stellar youth-
produced investigative news stories.[2] Soep has studied the sort of assessment
or critique that students experience in reflecting on their works in progress:

> Critique is making judgments about work. In an organic process,
> critique happens along the way; it becomes a property of learning,
> as opposed to something that evaluates the end result. It rises up as a
> resource and becomes an engine in moving the work forward. When you
> look at the language that happens in critique, it is very forward-looking.
> It projects a future for the work that is being produced. There
> is something really important about that, in the sense that what I am
> doing is going to matter to me and to this community of producers and
> to our imagined audience. This speaks to the fact that assessment is
> something that can feed forward, instead of just feeding back.[3]

The notion of actively feeding forward rather than passively receiving
feedback is key. The arts invite an attention to process that is all about how to
move forward with one's particular work or overall production in a medium.
It is not about an evaluation of good/better/best or a count of the number of
mistakes that have been found in your product. Within the context of attention to process in the arts, mistakes are not viewed as dead ends; they, too, feed
forward as opportunities for new or revised direction. Coming to a work of art
with an eye to what to do next, the artist must ask, as painter Jack Levine was
known to, "What's wrong here?" You have to work around what's right. What's
wrong: "That's a place to begin."[4] A New York City 1960s art teacher was
famous for challenging students: "Every mistake is on purpose. Figure it out."

Just like the young child who responds to a slip of a crayon as a new pos- ·
sibility in a drawing, the student of the arts can re-envision unsatisfactory as a
place of possibility. A West Coast acting teacher points out:

> Where else in these young people's lives do they learn that failure is not
> only constructive, but is sometimes the only way to move forward. An
> artistic enterprise's outcome is always uncertain, and that uncertainty
> has the power to let adolescents find virtue in things they thought
> they disliked about others, and perhaps disliked about themselves. The

strength of the ensemble built by an artistic endeavor carries over in positive ways to other aspects of the student artist's life in a way, say, an A in chemistry doesn't.

An attention to process is as evident in the high school music studio, where another teacher says the most important thing he teaches his ensemble is:

> Give yourself permission to fail . . . Learn to laugh. Explore and discover. Be respectful of one another's process. Set short-term goals for yourself so that you provide yourself with more opportunities to succeed. You are only as good as your last rehearsal. I always try to end each rehearsal and class with a question. Students should always have a reason to come back to a class. I ask questions in hope that they return searching for answers and sharing them with [the rest of us].

In a beginners' sculpture class in another independent high school, students were capturing movement in clay, working with wire armatures and an oil-based clay medium that would not harden or be fired. On this account, their work was entirely process-based, directed toward a product that would end up wedged back in a bucket of clay.

Nonetheless, students worked diligently on their pieces, capturing subjects that ranged from a cartoonish baseball player hitting the ball to a graceful caped character taking off in flight. "You need another hour on these," the teacher instructed as class ended and homework was assigned. The students nodded knowingly even as I wondered what more they would select to add to their well-developed pieces. They seemed to understand that the "homework" and the "lesson" were about the doing and refining, not the completion of work to display for others.

Reflection: How Am I Doing?

The process-oriented interaction between the maker and the work is interactive, with discovery and intention responding to and inviting shape and direction. A junior whose passion is physics but who values his work in the arts was "in" on such back-and-forth rapport. He spoke to me of the difference between physics and art: "I cannot talk to my physics book, but I can to my artwork." It is the same dialogue in a different frame that we described in terms of interpretation of another's work of art. In the process of making, the student is in conversation with his or her own work, considering its ideas and composition as if it were the work of another, and reflecting on its evolving status. That conversation is waged not with closed finished-product language like "good" or "bad" but with open questions and objectives that fuel progress and learning.

The junior who said he "couldn't talk to his physics book but he could to his art" explained that making art was more about a relationship than "traditional performance," more about an ongoing back-and-forth than a race to a measurable outcome. A violin student told me that when she is in private lessons with her teacher, the teacher "doesn't need to tell me when I have to start over." She is performing and reflecting on her performance all at once, and she knows for herself what she needs and wants to refine.

Consider yet another master class, this time as an example of the skilled use of process-based inquiry and reflection negotiated between a master arts teacher and his professional student:

Seated stage left in the tiny Los Angeles studio, the classically trained actor playing Dustin Hoffman's role (Ratso Rizzo) in a scene from the movie *Midnight Cowboy* looks as if he's about to cry. Six rows of students follow his moves. The air is charged, the room is silent, and, with a stare into nowhere, the intense young thespian paralyzes his audience by speaking his lines with a trembling and terrified voice: "I've been falling down a lot lately. I don't think I can walk anymore." His eyes cloud; his tone softens: "I'm scared."

"What was your objective—for that moment and for the scene overall?" the master class teacher asks, breaking the silence. Clearly accustomed to such directed queries (he asks similar questions of himself), the actor articulates his intention and ponders its relative success. He was determined, he explains, to gain the other character's attention and assistance. Furthermore, he thinks he had "something going" at the moment of interest. "Which part of it? When?" the teacher probes.

Through a series of focused questions and reflections, coach and actor entertain the possibility that the delivery of the line may have been sentimental; they weigh alternative options and brainstorm further the character's motivations; they don't agree. The teacher suggests they "play" with an alternative, and within minutes the scene is completely reconstructed. This time the actor is almost defiant in his admission of fear. The teacher finds this delivery more plausible; the actor embraces aspects of his original interpretation. Whatever the outcome, the redrafting of the scene has raised new possibilities for revision. The next version will raise more.[5]

The distinction displayed in this exchange is a clear example of the difference between evaluation as the judgment of right or wrong and assessment as inquiry and reflection in which the artist assesses: objectives ("What was your objective?" "I wanted to gain attention and help."), methods ("Did your emotional rendering achieve that end?" "What if you tried it a different way?"), and next steps ("What more or less or other do I want to do next?"). The actor and the teacher are mutually respectful colleagues, and the actor student is willing to honor the teacher's suggestion. But in the end the performance is his to consider and revise. And he will continuously.

The process orientation of the arts, associated as it is with ongoing self-assessment (How am I doing? What will I do next?) lies a territory apart from the standardized tests that evaluate product (How did I do? What did I do wrong?). While the ability to perform well on tests is a skill worth developing (and experience with taking tests may be the best preparation), the ability to self-assess purposefully may have more usefulness in that real world to which high school students and those who have left high school refer.

The ability to see a mistake as a place to begin rather than a point against you has implications for learning in any setting. A process orientation may indeed provide an opportunity for contextualizing performance on standardized tests. What if, instead of test performance being the absolute measure of student learning, teacher performance, and school effectiveness, it were one of the many elements taken into consideration in authentic ongoing self-assessment? If the tests were a part of process reflection (like the effectiveness of gesture in an overall consideration of a dramatic performance) and considered as opportunities for forward motion (what information do they provide for my further development?), how might they enrich rather than diminish innovative classroom activity?

What if the adults who had dropped out of high school had been better able to assess their overall process when their numerous absences were stacking the deck against them? Where am I now in this? What is my immediate objective? My overall objective? How are my methods getting me there? What do I have to do to move forward? What if I change this part of what I'm doing? How will it affect the whole?

Arts learning turns our attention to the doing even as or because the product will be inscribed with the effort. "If I focus more on the center of this movement, or image, or gesture, perhaps I can better achieve my goal?" If I focus more on the challenges the early settlers faced (challenges perhaps like those I face), might I be better able to engage with what was assigned in American History? Right or wrong answers speak to students of a win-or-lose world. But adolescents are making sense of a more complex reality, filled with life-and-death choices but also with everything in between. They need the skills of inquiry and reflection that the arts conspicuously provide so that they can make sense of the apparent right and wrong, the apparent lose and win, and the suffer and soar with which they are surrounded.

As a 19-year-old student told me, "I enjoy my art classes more than my other classes because instead of being lectured to, I am having a discussion with my images." That back-and-forth between process and product as it is envisioned and ultimately executed: "I really enjoy the process: coming up with the idea, sketching it out, talking about it, editing, and executing. While having the finished product is lovely, no one knows how hard you worked on it but you."

Making art and making sense of art extends beyond the "hard work" of the particular encounter to a new way of seeing the world. Manchester Craftsmen's Guild CEO Bill Strickland explains it as the process of "seeing your environment."[6] He explains that once a teenager has had the experience of taking a photograph, considering what he or she will include in the composition of the image, what light to reach for, what focus to achieve, she begins to consider other things in her world with similar attention. "I never looked at a salt shaker like this or a bridge, but since I stopped and took the time to take a picture of the bridge and to think about it, I realize that the object that I stopped to take a look at has significance."

A photography student in an independent day school reported the same phenomenon: "The camera facilitates and changes the way I look at everything around me. You start noticing the light. You start framing things that you learn to appreciate." A visual arts teacher who taught introduction to drawing in a public high school asked students to go outside and observe and draw, and "one particular student said after doing that exercise she has noticed the amazing spectrum of green out there and she said, 'My goodness, I never noticed how much there is I take for granted that is beautiful and worth noting in the world.'" Another of his high school students told him that "going through the process and skills to really look at something—man, I can go anywhere and look intelligently at something."

In light of the fact that students who leave school report a lack of interest and relevance in their classes, we need to consider what role they themselves might play in repairing that situation. Would a deeper involvement in the process of their learning, a keener attachment to the significance of what they see and experience, predispose them to make a difference in their own experience of learning? "This is about me—what I want to achieve, what I need to get to be the person I want to be and to do what I want to do in this world." An attention to process puts students in the role of making judgments from within, realizing their own potential to assess their own progress, ask the questions that will make the difference, and reflect with careful attention on their circumstance and direction.

Quincy Mosby, who had dropped out of school at 18, described (in a Youth Radio story put up on NPR) some of the factors at play in his leaving school, ". . . like the kids who stole from me or didn't bother waiting till my back was turned to tear me apart . . . So I started cutting and when you're getting up in age, you realize there's a world outside your house." By senior year, this young man was not going to school at all. "Dealing with teachers and getting work done is tiresome. There's something liberating about leaving school whenever you want." Finally, a brother-like mentor helped motivate him to see objectives and turn his life around:

> Once I decided I needed direction, it was easy to envision a path for myself. I'm getting my high school diploma, and I'm writing and drawing, exploring my artistic talent. I'm not a failure, not because I always succeed but because I'm too much of a loser to stop trying until I win.[7]

Engagement in the artistic process allows young people to understand that learning and achieving rely on the persistence to examine one's own journeying and to reflect on what one needs to succeed. A theater teacher put it well:

> In the arts class, failure is not a bad thing and there is not a strong need for students to be "right." There is a great lesson in the exploration, and results are not framed as such, for it is the process that is the lesson.

A high school dance instructor explained the positive approach to failure in her classroom:

> I think they appreciate that there are fewer "right" answers in dance and, therefore, fewer opportunities to be wrong or feel "stupid" in front of

their friends. On the other hand, I think my students appreciate very much how we handle everyday failures in the studio—the freedom to experiment, and the freedom to make a miserable mess of things.

Students seem vividly aware of the implications of their involvement at the center and in charge of the artistic process for their lives beyond school. One 9th-grader explained:

> I think the most important thing that I have learned in art classes is to believe in yourself. Intuition leads to brilliance. Go where the path follows—whether it's how the landscape of your imagination will play out on the canvas or what life path you will follow.

We need to encourage students to see that scores on tests are indicators, not determinants. It is not just with very young children that there is confusion over "Excellent" describing a particular effort and not an identity. That art teacher who declared that every mistake was on purpose ("figure it out") invited students to look at what they felt was off with what they were doing (carefully reflect) and to problem-solve (ask questions that would generate new effort) their way to new directions.

A process orientation is about considering, selecting, and pursuing the options that arise from close reflection and self-assessment. A high school music teacher encourages her students to "listen" carefully to their performances and to those of others and to keep close their skills of "critical thinking, imagination, and creativity." With close attention to the individual student, she tells me:

> I try to encourage a student's growth as an individual and help them to develop "life skills" (problem-solving, working with others, reframing a challenging situation, accepting their best effort) reflected in music study.

More Pleasure in Going to School

Bruno, a 25-year-old who dropped out of high school at 17, is only sorry he did not go on to college. But he does regret that there was no one at his high school with whom to explore options: "It would have been nice if there were more people—just somebody there who could recognize why I was pissed off and not just left me to my devices. If someone could have understood what I wanted to achieve and helped me to realize how some of the classes I didn't want to take would have helped me to get where I wanted to get."

Bruno is an adult spoken-word poet whose decision to leave high school was supported by his parents. The only caveat was that he needed to take the GED as soon as possible and not look for a job until he had passed. Having already passed his state's version of the 10th-grade math and English competency tests, Bruno was able to earn the GED easily that summer. In a homogenous suburban community, Bruno had always felt different. His town celebrated sports heroes while he preferred to write and read poetry. At 12, he began to attend poetry slams outside of school.

Bruno tells me that there was lots of peer pressure and bullying in middle school, but by the time he reached high school, he was not a person other kids wanted to "mess with." A large, well-built young man with an expansive, kind presence, he says that in high school he was a "troublemaker," outspoken and "kind of hostile about disliking school." By 9th grade, he had "formed a crew" with a group of like-minded kids who were "unabashedly different—outlandish" in their dress and manner. He got behind in a number of assignments and was often distracted in class.

While Bruno had "a few really good" English teachers who seemed to sense that he was capable (one of them he said "secretly" gave him an A on a story he'd written), when he walked out of class leaving behind an acidic poem about the battle of high school, he was put into an alternative education situation ("a separate school apart from real school for kids who weren't fitting in") where he was very limited in what he could do. At a time when outside of school he was winning prizes for his poetry, participating in his city's first slam poetry team, and selected to compete in Nationals, at school he was placed in an elementary English class where he was being taught "to write an introductory paragraph."

That class placement was the last straw for Bruno, but he had felt encouraged to leave high school from the time he arrived in 9th grade. His voice trembles as he tells me of a time when he and his friends were hanging out in the halls after detention speaking more loudly than they should have. When the vice principal came along, he referred to them as a bunch of "maggots" and asked them why they were still hanging around, why they wouldn't just go ahead and drop out. "I was called a maggot," Bruno repeats quietly, as if that one humiliating phrase captured his entire high school experience. For Bruno, school was "never a place where I could gain knowledge that I needed and I didn't want to accept the knowledge that the teachers were trying to give me."

Bruno feels that including the arts in the high school curriculum would help kids like him to stay in school. He thinks that students would take "more pleasure in going to school, have more incentive if they knew it was a valid place where their passions could be nurtured—not a miserable place like it was for me."

English class was as close to an arts class as Bruno ever had in high school. But when I asked Bruno when he first decided that he was an artist, he told me without hesitation that it was in 4th grade when he wrote a five-line poem on veterans not wanting to return to war. "A teacher published one of my poems in an anthology, and when she read it aloud, she cried. I wasn't the most gifted athlete, or the funniest, smartest student, but the teacher had no choice but to recognize me."

Bruno was invited recently to perform his poetry at a fundraiser for one of the new arts programs that has been put in place at his former high school. He was astonished and delighted to see that the arts were now everywhere; all students were required to take at least a full year of foundational arts. Where there had been no theater program, now there were two new stages; there was a beautiful music room and a new wing for visual arts classes that he remembers had been held in a hall.

"Right after I left this happened," Bruno exclaimed with outraged delight. "When I was in school, trying to find mutual spirits was hard while now there were dozens of students on stage making wonderful art. It was incredible." He felt that the school had been transformed and that the injustices he and others felt would be unthinkable in the current arts-filled environment.

Bruno runs a weekly open-mike poetry session at a local tavern, and he tells me about a guy his age who came up to him late in the evening after Bruno had performed a few poems. The "guy was trashed and crying" and he said to Bruno, "Don't you remember me? I treated you like shit in high school. With a few of my friends who played football, we beat you up regularly. But I have to tell you I write poetry. I always have and I did then but I was afraid to tell anyone." Bruno was overwhelmed by this revelation. His former tormentor went on: "Now I just want to know how I get to do what you do."

I asked Bruno how he responded to this statement, and he told me he made that artist connection between human beings that is the subject of the next chapter. "I gave him a hug," Bruno explained. "After all, in spite of their unalienable aggression, bullies are human and art is a good way to shake that up."

CHAPTER 5

CONNECTION

Winterfest Music Performance

Photograph by Phyllis Bretholz

"I felt so small and then I joined the orchestra . . ."

In the basement of the main building in a suburban high school, I slip into the overcrowded music studio. I am shoulder to shoulder with a young man on the slide trombone, and I am surprised by the enormity of the sound and the intimate size of the room. At least 20 musicians stand on elevated tiers and follow the direction of their deeply engaged music teacher, Mr. Knight. They are belting out a lively version of Glenn Miller's "In the Mood" and Mr. Knight has encouraged them to try to get through it all just once.

I am always intrigued by the stops and starts in the process of music rehearsals, how everyone seems to be moving along perfectly, and suddenly everything just sort of dissolves and ends. Mr. Knight is not fazed by these turns in the group's progress, and his confidence and energy are infectious. In spite of the bumps in the road, the joint is jumping here and these students are having fun. "Fun"—that word that arts advocates know as a hallmark of arts learning but dare not use too frequently for fear of its association with nonessential, i.e., extracurricular learning, versus the "hard work" of the mainstream.

I notice that in a group of go-getters, the drummer seems reluctant. Mr. Knight shares that she is unfamiliar with reading music, "as student drummers often are." These young musicians have their eyes fixed on their director. They seem unaware and uncaring about which of them hits the wrong note that makes them have to start again. They come from different grades, they have different levels of experience and skills, and they will go in different directions when they leave that room. But for the time they are there rehearsing, they are a tightly connected unit, joined together by Glenn Miller, Mr. Knight, and the music they are sending into the air.

Engagement: I Care

The human connection that the arts provide can be literal: the sense of community formed by the orchestra, the drama club, the atelier of adolescent artists drawing manga (Japanese-style comic book art) in somebody's basement, or the band cutting a CD in a local garage. An arts teacher and administrator remembers her experience of connection in her drama class in high school:

> We were a community like I had never experienced in school—accepting, deeply concerned for each other's well-being, and all on the same page

about the appeal of a dramatically lived life. I know our teacher and the drama games/training, too, had everything to do with creating that kind of bond.

The notion of ensemble is the experience of being involved in and dedicated with others to a production that, taken as a whole, is larger than the sum of its individual parts. A veteran arts teacher of high school–age students explained, "The arts seem to me to present a unique opportunity to unite. The challenge of a group project (be it a stage play, a newspaper, a video project, or a mural) builds an ensemble out of adolescents who otherwise would be hard-pressed to find common ground."

The head of the music department in an independent secondary school explained:

Teenage social needs and learning how to work with others can be accomplished through ensemble work. This can be readily seen in band, orchestra, choir as well as chamber music, soloist and accompanist, etc.—in fact, just watching the music students hang out in the music building is evidence of this "membership" in the world of the arts. (I know this happens in the other arts building as well.)

Lucy, a high school junior, remembered her first experience of her competitive high school. She knew no one and was pretty sure she had the wrong clothes, would never make friends, and would face a lonely existence in the library trying to keep up with "all the homework." She "felt small and couldn't be confident," but there was her clarinet and she'd enjoyed participating in the middle school orchestra. Among a throng of young musicians "who were much better than me," Lucy tried out and landed a chair in the school orchestra.

Suddenly she was coming to school early to practice, receiving guidance from upperclassmen who had been playing longer, feeling needed and as if she had a place. "I'll never be the best," she told me, but "I'm home here." I had the opportunity to speak to Lucy's teacher, who allowed:

Lucy may now claim that she is not much of a musician, and indeed, she is not an advanced clarinetist, but she is truly a success story in many ways . . . Throughout her three years here, she moved from the very last chair of the third clarinet section in the band to the assistant principal chair of the first clarinet section and is obviously a role model for those students who need to see what hard work and commitment can accomplish.

Jeanine, a friend of Lucy's, concurred and said of playing her flute: "Music was one of the ways that I could make friends and prove myself and shape my identity." These students' experience of immediate connection with a world of others with whom they work to create the best performance of music that they can resonates throughout the natural community-building connections that arts learning affords. A theater teacher explained:

> The act of performing as a company builds a sense of ensemble and community as students must cooperate to give a complete presentation, improving their ability to empathize and trust each other.

The range of electronics with which high school students stay in touch is staggering. Bruno had told me that it was bad enough a decade ago to be pushed around in front of four of your friends, "in front of your 750 friends of friends on Facebook, it's unimaginable." Bruno raises the exception of when "you share your poetry or images of your work on FB or tapes of your performances on YouTube." But that's about as far as you can get from the safe haven of the arts classroom, where critique is modeled and directed toward improvement.

Without minimizing the anguish caused or the love relationships forged online, it is important to distinguish between "getting" or "staying in touch" and the sort of "connecting" that the arts provide. Students are staying in touch (where I'm going, what I'm doing, how short I cut my hair) through electronic media, but they are not connecting in the way works of art connect us to the eternal themes and challenges of humankind and to one another, all of us struggling independently and together. A high school dance teacher tells me that in dance,

> Kids who sit in cubes get up and hold hands with the folks next to them, reaching out beyond their own small little spheres, and [they] make connections. And that is a remarkable thing to feel physically connected and make a physical bridge. For high schoolers that is so potent when you are learning your body and your "sexual stuff" and how you get connected in the community. These are huge things.

At its core, the artistic process is particularly human. From the detail of images on walls in caves, to the universal expressive quality of young children's drawings, to the staying power of a work of art that is treasured through the ages, the arts speak from and to our basic humanity. When we see a production of a classic play, there is a palpable connection between the audience (the viewers of the work) and the characters and the struggles portrayed on stage (the artistic content) and the playwright who wrote the script and others who bring it to life (the artistic creators).

Beyond that, however, there is a connection between the viewer and every other viewer who has ever made sense of the work. We imagine and feel connected to others who have seen this play or read that book or studied this painting or felt exhilarated as we do by this piece of music. We are joined by the content of the works, the human pleasures and perils that persist even as they assume different shades of meaning and relevance at different times and places throughout the life of the work. It is a cultural continuum—that human connection that fuels and frames our individual worldviews and our shared humanity.

The cultural connection that infuses the arts attaches us to our humanity and invites us to think about the feelings and ideas expressed in a work—those we have and represent in our own work, and those aroused by another artist's work. This powerful connection is consuming; it engages students in the artistic process and connects them to the world of others that makes art so compelling.

The learning outcome of engagement (I care) is singular for the arts and awakens in students a palpable sense of awareness and social responsibility (I care about others). As philosopher Maxine Greene expressed it:

> Wide-awakeness frees us to see more—the grass, the trees, the city streets, the abandoned ones, the homeless ones, the broken windows, the redesigned museum, what is absent and what is realized . . . to discover not only possibility, but to find the gaps, the empty spaces that require filling as we move from the is to the might be to the should be . . . to become more present to those around, perhaps to care.[1]

An experienced visual arts teacher in an urban high school considers the most important aspect of arts learning that it "raises awareness of social issues and democracy through community art projects such as mural-making." She tells the moving story of a man who arrived to fix a window:

I recognized the face of the man standing there. It was Rupert, a former student of mine from the Regional High School. The last time we saw one another was about seven years ago, at the funeral of another student, Jim, who was shot in a drive-by shooting. Since that time, Rupert got his GED, has a trade, an apartment and a car. While he was still in school, he worked on . . . a program that had students transform an abandoned crack house about a block away from the school, into what is now a place to live for homeless teenagers. Students were paid minimum wage and got course credit. The program gave students hard hats and tool belts and taught them electrical wiring and sheetrocking. During that time, I taught the group how to paint panels on 3' x 5' wooden boards to cover the open windows. After the building was completed, Rupert and a few others organized a mural in honor of Jim. Rupert told me that the panels we painted inspired him and the program director to paint this memorial.

For students who have the opportunity to make and/or perform works of art, there is the experience as well of a connection with other makers of art, individual artists, the local communities of artists, and beyond that to artists in the global community. Indeed, high school students tell us that the fact that their teacher is an artist, a veritable working representative of the community of artists beyond school walls, increases the draw of connection between student and teacher and sets the stage for a mutually respectful relationship.

Jonathan is a 16-year-old junior who loves everything about theater, from writing plays to lighting and sound to performing roles. He described his arts teachers as more passionate than teachers of other subjects. He told me, "A lot of teachers that I've had are not particularly passionate—it's just a class for them. For arts teachers, it's a life for them. They are teaching a class in it because they know what is up." He explains:

Artist teachers have used the arts to impact their lives and they have chosen to incorporate the arts into their lives and they have found it as a very important outlet for anything. They want to help people go through the same experience that they did. You don't talk about tests in an arts class but if you did it would be a "test of you as a person."

Jonathan is impressed that his theater teacher is "actually a director who works on a bunch of stuff and he also teaches theater. I'm not sure which is his primary job but both mean a lot to him." The legitimacy of the real-world experience—the realization that the teacher is a working artist himself, modeling day-to-day what professionals do—has great meaning for students.

We are reminded of the teacher of the arts mentioned earlier who advised that the most important aspect of his relationship with students, an element that many other art teachers have evoked, is to "treat them all as potentially future colleagues." This collegial equity sets a special tone, perhaps unlike that which students experience in other classes—an atmosphere in which mutual regard makes risk-taking possible, and shared passion electrifies the room.

A 10th-grader says of his arts teacher, "He has such a passion for theater and that adds so much to the class. Other teachers sometimes seem disinterested. But Carlos throws himself into the class." Lydia, a senior who studies violin, adoringly describes the experience of learning from a performing artist as a "special kind of student-teacher bond. They are like experts in their field and they are so godly . . . and you hope to get better, to be a better musician like your teacher."

"If you bring your passion into the room," Dennis, a secondary school dance (modern, tap, and ballet) teacher tells me, "kids are going to follow your passion. I go in every day and teach my passion." Dennis was a promising performer until a physical impairment brought his career onstage to an end. Seated with me outside the dance studio of the independent school where he teaches, Dennis shrugs and says, "I always expected to be a teacher. It just happened sooner than I expected."

Dance in his own high school experience was a godsend for Dennis. At the arts academy that Dennis attended, he was "just full of energy and life and couldn't sit still." Explaining further, he gives it a name: "Attention Deficit Hyperactivity Disorder." But thanks to the intense engagement he felt in his dance classes (I care), he could maintain focus longer than in academic classes, and what his teachers called "all that energy and intelligence" were brought together productively. For Dennis, dance helped him to harness his abundant energy to work "for him and not against him." It also helped him to do better in his academic classes, he says, because "It gave me a place where I felt really comfortable so I had that to fall back on." That safe haven again.

It matters that the connection among teachers of art (many of whom are working artists) and the "real" or professional world of the arts is authentic. It makes the connection between what students are studying in the art room and what they would need to know to pursue careers in the arts particularly vibrant. The lack of relevance ("why would I ever need what they are teaching") is a top reason for losing interest and leaving school offered by those who drop out. If spoken-word poet Bruno had had the opportunity to study poetry-writing with a professional poet (or at all), perhaps he would have had more patience with learning to write an introductory paragraph. A caring mentor might have been able to remind him of all the prose that poets are required to muster even as their passions lie in the creating and performing of their poetry.

Most basic, of course, is the introduction of the idea that the world of the arts offers viable careers for those who care to pursue them. This is an important realization for those students who feel they have a calling in the arts and for others who will or should one day be consumers of culture in the broader community. Some advocates believe that an incipient devaluation and mistrust of the arts as valuable professional options keep schools from including, let alone featuring, them in the curriculum. Artists are perceived as outsiders (something, as mentioned earlier, that may in itself provide connection to disenchanted adolescents) who selfishly create on their own without regard for others and with no hope of ever supporting a decent lifestyle. These concerns are misguided on two counts.

On the first count, reality gives the lie to the myth of the selfish, isolated artist. Examples abound of artist activists offering their talents to help raise money for worthy causes and/or stepping forward with positive action when others will not. A wave of community art centers that focus on education emerged in the 1960s from the efforts of artists (as teachers and administrators) who stepped forward to fill the void left by cuts in in-school arts education.[2] Second, the reality is that in our media-filled world, there are job opportunities, and some extremely lucrative ones, for individuals trained in a range of disciplines of and related to the arts.

It is necessary for arts advocates to lift the chip (the "sequoia," a friend calls it) that weighs on our shoulders and holds us to a defensive position from which we need always to "prove to them" that the arts are as good as other subjects and as worthy as other societal options for young people who love them. In this book, as in my earlier advocacy manifesto,[3] I have tried to focus on what it is that the arts themselves provide, and to give those who have not considered these features a chance to know them better. Surely in the spirit of the connection that arts learning extends, it would serve us well to reach out to "them" (however that otherness is construed) and demonstrate the respect and reception that we would hope for.

In that light, Marcus, a theater teacher in a small Midwestern town, described the gift of the realization that he could make a life in the arts:

> I had my first drama teacher when I moved to a small town in sixth
> grade. I was always a shy child, so acting and studying theater changed

my life as a chance to interact with other people, with the permission to be anything or anyone I wanted to be. In my small town, becoming an adult usually meant becoming an accountant, a police officer, a construction worker, or a teacher. Becoming a performing artist didn't seem like a serious option for a long time, but my [high school] teacher gave me the encouragement I needed to consider it as a career. Ultimately, it was my peers and community that convinced me. Once I saw how the entire town came together to put up a show in our gym auditorium, I knew I wanted to pursue a life in the theater to unite people through the power of a shared experience.

Responsibility: I Care About Others

"Uniting people through the power of a shared experience": That intrinsically connective quality of art-making and learning. Due to its incorporation of all of the earlier-mentioned features, connection is most naturally the last that I propose. All aspects of the arts generate unique learning opportunities. For students of high school age, connection may have special significance. Students at this perilous juncture are on the often lonely quest for individual place and in great need of support from a community of others.

I recently had the opportunity to experience what Marcus described: "The entire town came together to put up a show in our gym auditorium." In a small New England town, on a frozen winter night, the local university put up in its auditorium a production of *Peter Pan*[4] that featured 80 performers backed up by at least that many folks painting sets, designing and making costumes, and doing tech and publicity for the show.

The 80 performers were schoolchildren from kindergarten through high school, music theater majors from the university, local heroes like shopkeepers and restaurateurs, and assorted elders, several of whom have replaced their former work lives with active participation in community theater throughout the region. Teachers and students, friends and relatives, crowded the stage and the seats of the auditorium.

The show ran for two evenings and two matinee performances and each one of them was sold out. The evening that I saw the show, a retired local principal who supported the effort was being honored. Beyond the seated full house, standing room on all sides of the theater was filled with admiring teachers from the many years and schools where he had worked. The link between the arts and education was palpable on so many levels.

In preparation for the performance, local teachers and parents had read aloud to their children the story of *Peter Pan*: the boy who never grew up and regularly collected from their dream-filled beds real-world children whom he would teach to fly with him to Neverland (his/their world of make-believe). A teachers' conference was organized on the last day of the performance and teachers (from all levels and disciplines) from all over the state gathered around integrative arts activities that explored the elements of the James Barrie story, Victorian England, education at that time, and the themes of the play from the mechanics of flying to the moral implications of piracy. They shared ideas for process drama, poetry, puppetry, and collage.

I was intrigued to think that high school students might readily explore Barrie's oft-challenged fascination with childhood and the implications of his two heroes, an impish/courageous Peter and a foppish/fearful Captain Hook. Students who themselves are at the threshold of adulthood might understand the poignancy of Peter's refusal to pass through that gateway. "I won't grow up!" What, if any, are the purposes of imagination in the adult world? What limitations of childhood urge us to move on? I am uncertain as to whether directions like these were included in the various related curricula, but I experienced throughout it all (the show and the conference) the full vibrancy of an "arts-integrated" curriculum in which a single theme or artistic work is explored across curricula and media.[5]

The night of the performance was bitter cold, the snow was deep, and the nearest parking place left us walking at least a half mile to the auditorium. A buzz of anticipation radiated from audience members en route and in their seats in the theater. I had had the privilege as a child of seeing two Broadway productions of *Peter Pan*, one with Jean Arthur as Peter and Boris Karloff as Captain Hook, and the other with Mary Martin and Cyril Ritchard. These iconic figures brought the play to life with unforgettable mastery and style. Here in this frigid auditorium, with more people packed in than I thought could be allowed, with small children with winter coughs, older people (like me) keeping their warm coats at hand, mothers and fathers of the actors and the folks backstage, a 19-year-old student took the stage as Peter, and a teacher in his program played Mr. Darling and Hook. And they rocked.

A 13-year-old with a lovely voice played Wendy, the little girl Peter took to Neverland; a kindergarten child played her little brother and rode on the back of a big stuffed dog (the children's nanny), whose identity was never revealed but whose mother, I believe, was sitting right behind me. The web of connection held us all in, and it occurred to me that this production demonstrated in action all five features of the arts that I suggest make arts learning different from learning in other subjects and essential to our children's education:[6]

First, there is the tangible product, the work of art, the show itself that would not be there were it not for the efforts of so many individuals on and offstage, in the present and in the past. From the work itself, as asserted earlier, we learn about:

- *Imagination:* the realm of "what if." What if I could fly? What if I flew to an imaginary place? What would happen there? and
- *Agency:* the power of "I matter." I make a difference in the creation of something (the show) that was not there before I sang or danced or worked the lights.

Second, in the arts, as we have discussed, there is specifically a focus on emotion that gives us the opportunity to learn about:

- *Expression:* "This is how I feel." Let me show you through my performance of a worried Wendy what I know of fear and concern.
- *Empathy:* "This is how you/others feel." Look at how Peter's gang, the poor Lost Boys, longed for a mother. It must be hard not to (as it sometimes is to) have a parent.

Third, there is about the arts a deliberate ambiguity, a way in which many valid meanings (not one right or wrong answer) can be found in the work. And from this we learn about:

- *Interpretation:* "What I think matters." I wonder why the roles of the Father and Captain Hook are always played by the same actor. I believe that reflects suspicion of all grown-ups—perhaps that they all are pirates in one way or another.

But we also learn from ambiguity about

- *Respect:* "What others think matters." You may think the use of the same actor for the father and Hook demonstrates a kinder idea: that even grown-ups know how to play. That idea interests me. One of us is not right and the other wrong. We respect and can learn from one another's different views.

Fourth, the arts draw our attention to process, the doing that matters at least as much as the done—the rehearsing that is as important as the show. And a process orientation sets the stage for:

- *Inquiry:* questions that make use of information but go beyond right or wrong answers to considerations of what I want to know. "What ideas and emotions do I see expressed in this work?" "What is Captain Hook so afraid of?" "How will I incorporate my interpretation into my performance?" and
- *Reflection:* "How am I doing and what will I do next?" Purposeful self-assessment goes beyond closed judgments of good or bad to open considerations of revision. "Does what I do onstage reveal my intention as Captain Hook to hide my fears by terrifying others?" "Should my stance change when I hear the crocodile approach?" "How can I make my performance more effective?"

And finally, and this is everywhere evident in this community-wide production of *Peter Pan*, the arts feature connection: our connection to the other performers in the show, the connection between the audience and the players and the playwright, and all our connections to every performance of *Peter Pan* that we've ever seen or that others have seen throughout time as we are seeing this one today. A connection to our shared humanness necessarily invites:

- *Engagement:* "I care." The universal themes of lost youth and cherished imagination make the show absolutely compelling whether I am onstage performing or in the audience making my own sense of what is going on. "I am so passionate that I rise to my feet to let the actors to whom I have felt connected know how much I care."

And last, that attendant sense of social responsibility that the arts awaken:

- *Responsibility:* "I care for others." I care about the community of cast members and the broader community we all represent. I am responsible for my contribution onstage and in the broader world. I am inspired by *Peter Pan* to want to try to make it possible for all children to have homes of their own and to see beyond the given in their day-to-day lives.

From imagination to social responsibility, the arts teach our children about what it is to be human and enable them to experience their humanity in thought and action. Beyond the longings for childhood and Neverland, cherished works of art throughout time have addressed compelling social issues such as the injustices of poverty and the inequities of class or the human spirit's potential for inhumanity and abuse. The social injustices addressed in the artistic expressions of today are connected to those addressed throughout history not only because they reflect the continuum of inhumanity that challenges human beings, but because they demonstrate the timeless power of art to embody and convey these human dilemmas.

What do we do with our longings for idealized home? How do we adapt to adulthood when it seems more about loss than gain? How, in a ruthless world, do we perpetuate imagination? When doubters dare to trivialize arts learning, relegating timeless works (perhaps especially those as conspicuously playful as *Peter Pan*) to the sidelines of our students' experience, let us draw attention to the content of works of art and the many capacities their study awakens for students of all ages.

While Shakespeare's *Romeo and Juliet*, Nathaniel Hawthorne's *The Scarlet Letter,* and Sapphire's *Push*[7] may provide more obviously resonant templates for reproduction and reinterpretation in the lives of contemporary adolescents, let us not forget the power of any work that has lasted throughout time to awaken our children to their connection to their own cultures, the cultures of others, and the greater Culture of humankind. [8]

Connection was the subject of a 16-year-old sophomore's explanation of his love for theater. Jacob knew he was drawn to theater in the 6th grade, but it all came together in the 8th grade when he was cast as the Earthworm in his school's production of Roald Dahl's *James and the Giant* Peach:[9]

> I had always thought I was a visual artist because I liked to dump
> paint on canvas and mush it around making things look pretty but not
> thinking about outcomes. But I actually became the earthworm . . . I
> knew I wasn't just playing myself as the worm and I can see myself in the
> part . . . I have become the character and the character had become me
> and that is when I first saw myself as an artist.

Reflecting on the many parts he's had the chance to play since then, Jacob tells me that playing a part, "bringing it to life," is a "wonderful process." And it's all about the "connection—about the role becoming a part of me." A high school dance teacher describes that internal connection to one's own story: "If your parents are getting a divorce or you have some heartache, your dancing will connect you to your own story."

Jacob explains that he has "a special bond with everything I've done really... all the plays and things I've written—they become incorporated into your life. It's like living art. If I can find a connection, I go with it . . ." The connection to the arts can keep students who are at risk of leaving high school in school. A ballet teacher in an after-school program told me the story of Freddy:

> One student who stands out in my memory is "Freddy," who almost dropped out of high school because he did not see any value in the education he was receiving. He eventually started coming to school only for the dance classes, but when it was explained to him that he needed to satisfy the school's academic requirements to continue attending (and that the dance company director who had offered him a job would cancel his contract if he dropped out), he reapplied himself to his academic classes and ended up finishing on time.

A "serious singer" who has been singing in choirs since 3rd grade told me that she "felt so alone" in high school, but when she joined choir and the madrigal group, "everything came together" and she has become more independent in all her work because "I have a core on which I can rely." "Living art" seems an apt descriptor for the link across media, circumstance, and understanding that engagement in the arts provides.

The headmaster of a progressive arts-based high school sees the connection that the arts provide between students and the world as keeping them from shutting down and as opening the window for "real" moral education. In order for high school students to make sense of the world, he says, they need to have the chance the arts give them:

> to release what's inside—their interior world which they don't always grasp connecting to the world around them and if they have great experiences in the arts they are willing to take chances and to be expressive . . . and at this time when they are both adult and child uniquely in a way that they never will again . . . kids should be thinking about what the appropriate relationship should be with the rest of the world and how they should have some impact on the world and that they have a responsibility to the world.

The headmaster is speaking not of students who are singularly drawn to the arts or of those who are particularly talented. The connection to one's inner life is there for all students to experience. A high school visual arts teacher speaks of the transformation that the arts—just at the level of sheer pleasure—can provide:

> Time and time again I have witnessed a student rise from the awkward, unconfident, confused freshman to the poised, focused, and directed senior. One student, John, embodied this transformation and made a big impression on me as a teacher. John was not someone I would describe as naturally "gifted," nor particularly driven. He simply enjoyed making art and being in the studio more than being anywhere else in high school. John lost his father unexpectedly and at a young age, he was extremely tall and painfully shy, and he did not project confidence in any sense of the word. In art, none of this mattered. He could come to class and go about his business and for the most part, feel accepted. For him, art was a hobby . . . a pastime . . . an escape. I personally never experienced art so casually, because art has always been so central to my life. I never recognized art as simply, yet importantly, a diversion. For John, art offered a relaxing—though absolutely necessary—escape from the pains of his life. This idea, of art as escape, sounded cliché to me for many years, but seeing it play out for a teenager struggling to fit in and feel good about himself has helped me recognize the significance of the arts for this purpose.

An Interdisciplinary Nexus

The school day is fragmented (you go to the separate spaces reserved for science, math, etc.), but the arts provide an opportunity for students to come together and connect the various strands of their learning. This happens not only among the various strands of arts learning, but also across all subjects.

The school musical, for example, obviously brings together learning and students in the visual arts for set design, musical training for vocal and band performance, and theater mavens contributing dramatic expertise. But students doing tech theater are putting to use physics and mathematical concepts and acumen, just as the theater students are using the analytic skills they've acquired in their humanities classes to make sense of the script. Undoubtedly the entire ensemble has considered the history of the show, both when it first was done and how, as well as its impact on and reflection of the period in which it was first produced.

The arts provide a nexus for a range of disciplinary understandings. A musical composition, like a play, demonstrates psychological considerations in its expressive potential, historical considerations such as relevant styles and events, mathematical considerations in the relationship between notes and stanzas, and narrative elements in the unfolding of the story it tells. The arts connect disciplines not only by bringing disparate subjects together in a work of art, but also by their impact on individual domains. A sophomore who values his arts learning explains the connections he values between arts learning and real life and arts learning and other subjects:

> When am I ever going to use chemistry after this year or put to use my knowledge about Louis the Eighth and the silk trade? But I'll always need to know how to encapsulate a personality without becoming that character through and through . . . anything that requires "getting into" something is going to be assisted by the acting process. . . . Also, the arts are going to carry over and the other subjects are not going to so much . . . if you're a physicist, you can use the arts, a chemist who thinks about composition, an historian. Arts are the most important thing if not because they are so wonderful and rich but because they impact everything.

CHAPTER 6

WITH AN EYE TO THE FUTURE

University Educational Theatre Collaborative Production of *Peter Pan*

Photograph by John Anderson

"I must have a purpose . . ."

In arguing for an increase of arts education in high schools, I have tried not to place the arts in opposition to those courses that traditionally hold sway. Furthermore, even as I have contrasted the learning that students do in the arts with learning that can be more reasonably measured by standardized tests, I hope not to have disparaged either factual learning or standardized tests. These aspects of student learning are important. Students must know how to acquire information and how to use it in the formation of their own questions.

What I have challenged is the current prioritization of learning outcomes that can be measured on tests. The fact that something can be measured does not make it a priori more valuable than something else. At face, that may seem an obvious statement. Surely we value and categorize as beyond measure kindness, character, and a host of other human virtues. Why should it be so different in the education of what we hope will be motivated, caring, and responsible citizens? How can we demean learning writ large by pushing to the side those outcomes that defy measurement even as they perpetuate and expand our human potential?

Like the technical aspects of art-making, the quantitative aspects of all subjects must be taught and evaluated. They just cannot be all. We cannot reduce student learning to what we can count. We cannot reduce the artistry of classroom teachers to teaching for the test. And we cannot diminish the rich cultural priorities of all kinds of schools by valuing them only as far as test results prove worth. The tests need to be there, but as part of the greater whole—not as final judgment on the futures of students, teachers, and schools.

Bruno, who left school before his junior year, had passed the 10th-grade tests in English and math that his state required for a high school diploma. After leaving, he went on to pass the GEDs handily. Most of the adults who shared their experiences of dropping out of school had passing or better grades.[1] Was there nothing that Bruno missed by eliminating the 2 years that, in the end, he did not need to qualify him for work or college application? High school educations must be about more than the measurable. An increase in arts learning can illuminate and enrich the "more."

We need to remember that, like the students who leave them, our struggling schools, whether "dropout factories" or those being closed for not making the test benchmark, are not devoid of merit. Artful teachers work, often without recognition, at the center or in the margins even of poorly functioning schools. They persevere and find courage and inspiration in the knowledge that they have reached at least some of their students. This has always been true.

Today's right/wrong/win/lose attitude has positioned us to dismiss rather than investigate, to condemn rather than seek new direction, to punish rather than persevere. A disenfranchised 16-year-old put it crudely: "Grading just gets kids to stress over things that aren't really that important. If you do bad on something, they should help you learn how to make it better instead of failing your ass off." Educational historian Diane Ravitch spoke with more grace but equal passion with regard to schools:

> Good leadership in education means taking responsibility for making
> things better, rather than sitting back and monitoring how schools
> perform . . . Schools with low test scores are mostly schools that enroll
> large numbers of students who are struggling to keep up. Closing
> the school does nothing to help the students. District leaders should
> do whatever is necessary to help the school improve. . . . Educational
> euthanasia is unethical.[2]

It must be noted that just as artful non-arts teachers already strive to bring interest and relevance to their classrooms, not all art teachers realize the features and outcomes that the arts have the capacity to provide. In any discussion of reform, we should try not to polarize, but to remember, as one high school student told us of the interpersonal quality of arts learning, that "we are all in this together working to make something happen." We are striving to do the best we can for students who face challenges and pitfalls that didn't exist a quarter century ago.

Interest and Relevance

With an eye to interest and relevance in the high school setting, it is clear that interest infers student engagement in what is being offered. This can extend from the nature of the subject matter to the quality of teacher rapport. In this context, relevance is most frequently associated with readiness for job or college after graduation.[3] It can, however, and does here include relevance to the immediate lived lives of adolescents and to the personal challenges and growth that they face. "If only they knew who I was . . . my life now."

We began with the tangible object, the work of art, whether a drawing, poem, dance, or theatrical production. High school students and teachers tell us that having the freedom to envision the work (imagination) and the personal power to see it through to completion (agency) is a real draw. Students report that they experience most of their high school classes as teacher-directed, with students having little recourse for determining the content or presentation of the subject matter.

But in art classes, students experience their own centrality—mattering—at the helm of their production and learning. Beyond fostering student authority over the work they are creating, arts teachers promote this centrality by taking a collegial approach that respects the students' ultimate artistic autonomy. On this account, students feel that they are interesting to their teachers, and ultimately they seem to find that they are more interesting to themselves.

Overall, interest derives from the challenge of envisioning and creating something that was not there before the student conceived it. It keeps students engaged and taking responsibility for their work in their arts classes. Relevance lies in the autonomy that art making awakens. It contributes to the sense of competency that adolescents require in order to take charge and navigate the daunting passage from child to adult.

With regard to art's unapologetic focus on emotion, students are deeply interested and attached to the process of giving form to (expressing) their own emotions. They also welcome the chance to recognize and learn about the emotions of others (empathy). Adolescence is known as a period of intense feeling, deep sensitivity, stress, passion, egotism, self-sacrifice, and devotion.[4] On this account, students value the arts classroom as a safe haven for encounters with learning that is immediately relevant to their own personal development and growth.

Almost half the adults who had dropped out of high school reported that they did not have an adult to whom they could go with personal issues. Understandably, emotions can be intrusive in, for example, a math class where the teacher has a fixed teaching agenda around objectives that do not include expressivity.[5] In the arts classroom, however, there is room for addressing these issues through the work at hand. Employing various artistic media, students can give purpose and shape to the emotions that run high in their lives as young adults.

There are valued opportunities in theater to play a role and represent feelings and perspectives that are sometimes new to students. Students tell us that the visual arts allow them to express emotion that cannot be contained by words. They realize that even in ballet, where technique often appears as the ruling objective, it is in poignant expression that their dancing finds creativity and value. Interest and relevance abound again because of the arts' attachment and usefulness to the adolescent's developmental agenda: here, the trying on of roles and the exploration of one's own and others' emotions.

In the vivid muddy waters of ambiguity out of which the arts find power and clarity, students treasure the discovery of their own voices. They learn from the attendant skills of interpretation that they and others have perspectives worthy of respect. In the construction of meaning in response to works of art, students find new modes of inquiry that transcend right or wrong answers and lead to new and better questions. In this context, they can experience firsthand how useful facts can be to their individual interest in what they encounter.

High school students are at the ready to identify and consider as if they were their own the problems that artists set for themselves within and across media. Interpretation (analyzing and critiquing) and respect (for one's own ideas and those of others) are relevant to and of immediate use to students in their lives as consumers of visual media. They need to evaluate rather than to accept the stereotypes with which they are barraged and to put in perspective the power of media constructions. Arts education is replete with engaging opportunities for acquiring these relevant skills.

Arts teachers establish what students have called "a creative relationship in which you can formulate ideas together and take guidance from the teacher in the direction you have personally chosen." A view of your teacher as a co-constructor of ideas (rather than the holder and conveyor of knowledge) fosters the sense of self-respect and ability to find multiple meanings that students will need to find their way in the complex (gray, not black-and-white) adult world. Being treated as an adult responsible for one's own meaning-making is a heady experience. For students who are used to the drill of providing the answer that the teacher wants, it can be most challenging. Adults who dropped out of school suggest that they would have welcomed such high expectation.

Clearly relevant to the high school student's life (now and in the future) is what the process orientation of art can teach us about real assessment—not the grade or comment that says after the fact whether you were on or off target—but the kind of assessment that "feeds forward," enabling us to attend carefully to and continuously refine our course of action. In this context, mistakes are seen as generative, awakening new possibilities rather than leading to dead ends: "Failure is not only constructive but sometimes the only way to move forward."

The ability to self-assess is relevant to making one's way through the adult world, and it should also be helpful to students at risk of dropping out of school. If they can see beyond the sense of failure that contributes to their decision to leave, they may also be able to reconsider their current state as an opportunity for revision and forward motion. How might we encourage these young people to regard their lives as works in progress (perhaps even as works of art) in which they look to mistakes not for self-definition, but as places to begin?

The last feature, connection, may be the most obviously relevant to the lives of high school students. Adolescents who are struggling for self-definition, even as they long to belong to one group or another, are engaged socially and emotionally by the power of ensemble that fuels so much of artistic performance. The intense engagement in (attachment to) the co-construction of an artistic production awakens students to a sense of responsibility (to the group) that can extend beyond the work to the world of human issues represented in and through art.

Feeling oneself as the member of a tradition of caring, world-changing artists empowers young people to see beyond themselves to the needs of others and to acquire the sense of social responsibility that results in positive change. The connective aspects of arts learning awaken engagement and responsibility that are immediately relevant to adolescents' lives as members of a school community but beyond that to the greater community in which they will participate and to which they will contribute as adults.

In separating out features of the arts, as I have done, we cannot lose sight of that aesthetic whole that is greater than the sum of its parts. All five of the identified features (as well as the learning outcomes they generate) overlap and mutually inform one another. Indeed, it is interesting to move the outcomes around the features and consider, for example, a process orientation in terms of expression and empathy, or ambiguity in terms of imagination and agency.

The arts, we have noted, are naturally synthetic. A painting, for example, brings together psychology (in the human issues it addresses), history (in historical events represented or the art movement in history in which it partakes), math (in the proportions at play), chemistry (in the components of the materials), philosophy (in the timeless questions it proposes), and I could go on. This interweaving of disciplines provides a model for students who are struggling to make sense of their various courses.

Arts education (from the production of the tangible product to the pull of social responsibility) enables students to put the learning they do in separate classes together in cohesive and purposeful ways. In all these respects, the arts have the potential to add engagement to high school students' entire experience of school and to give it relevance to the whole that they are creating out of their lived lives.

What We Need to Do

Our high schools need to increase to the level of other core subjects (math, science, English, history, et al.) the amount of arts education credits required for graduation. These requirements need to apply to all students, not just those identified as bound for college. The increased requirement (and the esteem reflected therein) will give more adolescents the opportunity to experience the benefits of arts learning that the students who contributed to this work understand so well.

Resources need to be increased. We need more visual arts studios (for two-dimensional and three-dimensional media) and black-box theaters and practice rooms and ballet barres and musical instruments and computers for digital work and stages and galleries for display of student productions. And we need to increase the number of domain-specific (visual arts, music, ballet, drama, media, etc.) arts specialists on our high school faculties so that all students can learn from experts.

We need more visiting artists demonstrating in classrooms, mentoring students, and leading master classes in a range of artistic domains. We need more opportunities for field trips to cultural institutions, concert halls, and artist studios, more integration of arts learning into non-arts subjects, and more collaboration with the many wonderful arts learning institutions that exist beyond school walls. At base, we need the acceptance of arts education as a vital and essential part of student learning from 9th through 12th grade.

We inadvertently tell our students that their present realities as young people are not of significance. Even as they are developmentally poised to consider their futures, we consider the present for them as a means to an end. If they complete high school, they will get jobs that pay more or go to colleges that will enable them to earn even more and position them to make greater contributions to the world. This is true in public high schools, where school success is marked by the number of students who stay to graduate, and in independent schools, where success is measured by the list of colleges to which last year's senior class was accepted.

But for high school students to come to school and stay there day after day, there must be an immediate reason. As a high school visual arts instructor declared, "I must feel that I can learn something every day from my kids. Whether it is how to teach, coach, or mentor, I must have a purpose to teach every day." Certainly, high school students deserve the same draw: the knowledge that they will learn something every day from their teachers, that there is a purpose in their going to school every day.

As one high school student told us, the older you get, the more aware you are of "the world outside your house." I believe the call for interest and relevance on the part of former high school students addresses this need: "High school must engage me. It needs to have relevance to the life I am living and not just to the life that I will get to live if I make it through high school."

As I have hoped to show in these pages, arts education can help make the immediate experience of high school matter. Ask any graduate what they remember from high school and, as one student suggested, they will not discuss King Louis VIII and the silk trade. They will tell you of the time they played Captain Hook in the school musical (they may even sing their entire solo) or of the day their poem was read aloud in assembly or their collage of green hammers was in a school gallery on display. While I agree with Bruno that the arts can help make high school "a more pleasant experience," I believe further that the arts can give high school students a reason to attend and to stay in school.

NOTES

Introduction

1. See, for examples, Famous High School Dropouts: http://www.education-reform. net/dropouts2.htm and Noted Individuals-High School and Elementary School Dropouts: http://www.angelfire.com/stars4/lists/dropouts.html.

2. See for this, related data, and perspectives of young adults who have dropped out of high school as referenced throughout this text: *The Silent Epidemic: Perspectives of High School Dropouts,* March 2006, A Report by Civic Enterprises in association with Peter D. Hart Research Associates for the Bill and Melinda Gates Foundation by John M. Bridgeland, John J. DiIulio Jr., and Karen Burke Morison, http://www.civicenterprises. net/pdfs/thesilentepidemic3-06.pdf.

3. This recent report updates dropout rate decline from one-third to one-fourth of all students and reports on achievements in the heavily funded efforts to fight attrition in our schools: *Building a Grad Nation: Progress and Challenge in the High School Dropout Epidemic,* November 2010, A Report by Civic Enterprises, Everyone Graduates Center at Johns Hopkins University, America's Promise Alliance, written by Robert Balfanz, John M. Bridgeland, Laura A. Moore, and Joanna Hornig Fox. Sponsors: Target (lead), AT&T, Pearson Foundation, http://www.edweek.org/media/14grad1.pdf.

4. See *The Silent Epidemic,* pp. 3–4.

5. Ibid., p. 5.

6. See Davis, J. H., with Ackerman, J., Bernard, R., Brody, A., & Gatzambidés, R. (2001). *Passion and Industry: Schools That Focus on the Arts.* Cambridge, MA: President and Fellows of Harvard College.

7. The high school students and high school teachers of the arts that I interviewed for this work or who contributed written responses to questionnaires are cited with permission and are given pseudonyms or remain unnamed, as do their schools.

8. *Building a Grad Nation: Progress and Challenge in the High School Dropout Epidemic.*

9. *Staying in School: Arts Education and New York City High School Graduation Rates,* October 2009, A Report by the Center for Arts Education, by Douglas Israel, available at *http://www.cae-nyc.org/staying-in-school/arts-and-graduation-report.* And see the earlier report, *The Role of the Fine and Performing Arts in High School Dropout Prevention,* July 1990, A Curriculum Development and Renewal Project developed

by the Center for Music Research for the Florida Department of Education, Division of Public Schools done by Florida State University, Tallahassee, Center for Music Research, http://www.eric.ed.gov:80/PDFS/ED354168.pdf.

10. Refer for further explication to my recent books: *Why Our Schools Need the Arts* (Teachers College Press, 2008) and *Framing Education as Art: The Octopus Has a Good Day* (Teachers College Press, 2005).

11. Sizer, T. (1976). *Secondary Schools at the Turn of the Century.* Westport, CT: Greenwood Press (Original work published 1964 by Yale University Press), p. 69.

12. Korzenik, D. (1985). *Drawn to Art: A Nineteenth-Century American Dream.* Hanover, NH, and London: University Press of New England, p. 65.

13. Dow, A. W. (1899). *Composition: A Series of Exercises in Art Structure for the Use of Students and Teachers* (13th ed.). New York: Doubleday.

14. *From There to Here: The Road to Reform of American High Schools.* Issue Papers. The High School Leadership Summit. http://www2.ed.gov/about/offices/list/ovae/pi/hsinit/papers/history.pdf

15. See The Cardinal Principles of Secondary Education, prepared by Melissa Scherer, from Raubinger, F. M., et al. (1969). *The Development of Secondary Education.* New York: Macmillan, http://www.nd.edu/~rbarger/www7/cardprin.html.

16. Dewey, J. (1958). *Art as Experience.* New York: Capricorn (Original work published 1934), p. 73.

17. Lowenfeld, V., & Brittain, W. L. (1970). *Creative and Mental* Growth (5th ed.). New York: Macmillan. (First edition published 1947).

18. Efland, A. (1992). The Threefold Curriculum and the Arts. *Art Education, 49*(5), 49–56. And see Efland, A. (1990). *A History of Art Education: Intellectual and Social Currents in Teaching the Visual Arts.* New York: Teachers College Press.

19. Dobbs, S. M. (1997). *Learning in and through Art: A Guide to Discipline Based Art Education.* Los Angeles: The Getty Education Institute for the Arts.

20. Sizer, T. (1984). *Horace's Compromise: The Dilemma of the American High School.* Boston: Houghton Mifflin.

21. *From There to Here: The Road to Reform of American High Schools.*

22. And for a change in heart by a noted educational researcher, see Diane Ravitch, (2010). *The Death and Life of the Great American School System: How Testing and Choice Are Undermining Education.* New York: Basic Books.

23. See Murfee, E. (1995). *Eloquent Evidence: Arts at the Core of Learning.* Report by the President's Committee on the Arts and the Humanities. Washington D. C. And compare Winner, E., & Hetland, L. (Eds.). (2000). The Arts and Academic Achievement: What the Evidence Shows. *Journal of Aesthetic Education, 34*(3/4) pp. 3–6.

24. See Arts Education Partnership State Policy 2008 Database: Arts Requirements for High School Graduation, http://www.aep-arts.org/database/results.htm?PHPSESSID

=20d86ef0b9cc05627c7836b89e072fe2&select_category_id=32&search=Search, and Arts Education Partnership 2007–8 State Policy Survey-summary table of Results, http://www.aeparts.org/database/AEPSummaryTableofResults.pdf.

25. National Arts Education Association, Definition of Fine Arts for High School Graduation Requirements, http://www.arteducators.org/about-us/Definition_of_Fine_ Arts_for_High_School_Graduation_Requirements.pdf.

26. See Davis, J. H. (2010, Fall). Learning from Examples of Civic Responsibility: What Community Art Centers Teach Us about Arts Education. *Journal of Aesthetic Education, 44*(3), 82–95.

27. See Davis, J. H. (1997, Spring) Drawing's Demise: U-shaped Development in Graphic Symbolization, *Studies in Art Education, 38*(3), 132–157.

28. Edwards, B. (1979). *Drawing on the Right Side of the Brain.* Los Angeles: J. P. Tarcher.

29. Lawrence-Lightfoot, S. (1988). *The Third Chapter.* New York: Farrar, Straus and Giroux.

30. See Winner, E. (1988). *The Point of Words.* Cambridge, MA: Harvard University Press.

Chapter 1: Tangible Product

1. Stephen Sondheim (music and lyrics) and James Lapine (book), *Sunday in the Park with George* (1991). New York: Applause Theatre Book Publishers.

2. Personal communication, 1991.

3. See, for example, Zimmerman, B., & Cleary, T. (2006). Adolescents' Development of Personal Agency: The Role of Self-Efficacy Beliefs and Self-Regulatory Skill. In T. Urdan & F. Pajares (Eds.), *Self-Efficacy Beliefs of Adolescents* (pp. 45–60). Greenwich, CT: Information Age Publishing.

4. See *The Silent Epidemic*, p. 5.

5. Olsen, R. (2011). *Art, Kids, and Institutions: A Brief Memoir of Teaching.* San Francisco: Theoben Press, pp. 22–23.

6. Goodman, N. (1978). When Is Art? In *Ways of Worldmaking* (pp. 57–70). Indianapolis, IN: Hackett.

7. See the stages of famous epistemologist Jean Piaget, who observed that students of high school age, like adults, could perform what he called "formal operations," i.e., manipulating abstract concepts. For example, see his classic *The Language and Thought of the Child* (1926). New York: Harcourt Brace.

8. See Greene, M. (1995). *Releasing the Imagination: Essays on Education, the Arts, and Social Change.* San Francisco: Jossey-Bass, p. 125.

9. Davis, J. H., Soep, L., Remba, N., Maira, S., & Putnoi, D. (1993). *Safe Havens: Portraits of Educational Effectiveness in Community Art Centers That Focus on Educa-*

tion in Economically Disadvantaged Communities. Cambridge, MA: Harvard Project Zero, Presidents and Fellows of Harvard College, p. 42.

10. See *The Silent Epidemic*, p. iii.

11. Ibid., p. 8.

12. See Davis et al. (2001).

13. See Greene (1995), p. 150.

14. See Olsen (2011), p. 17.

15. Artist statement, http://www.cla.purdue.edu/waaw/Cohn/Artists/Lacystat.html.

16. Part 1: http://www.youtube.com/watch?v=SI6iYKTG98U; Part 2: http://www.youtube.com/watch?v=MqADLkxzgkE.

17. See *The Silent Epidemic*, p. 12.

18. See *Building a Grad Nation*.

19. See *Safe Havens*, p. 83.

20. For Pittsburgh school data, see the 2006 Rand Corporation study, *Estimating Graduation and Dropout Rates with Longitudinal Data: A Case Study of the Pittsburgh Public Schools,* available at www.rand.org. For information on the Guild, see http://mcgyouthandarts.org and Bill Strickland's inspiring book (with Vince Rause), *Make the Impossible Possible* (2007). New York: Doubleday.

21. See Davis, J. H. (2010).

22. See Heath, S. B., Soep, E., & Roach, A. (1998). Living the Arts Through Language Learning: A Report on Community-Based Organizations. *Americans for the Arts, 2*(7), 1–20.

23. In Caroline Abels, "Top 50 Cultural Forces in Pittsburgh with a Twist: No. 1 Bill Strickland," in Lifestyle post-gazette.com, June 2, 2002. http://www.post-gazette.com/life style/20020602strickland0602fnp3.asp.

24. Notably Diane Ravitch, *The Death and Life of the Great American School System: How Testing and Choice Are Undermining Education.* (2010). New York: Basic Books.

Chapter 2: A Focus on Emotion

1. See for related content Davis et al. (1994).

2. See for example, Erikson, E. H. (1950). *Childhood and Society.* New York: W.W. Norton).

3. http://www.urbandictionary.com/define.php?term=a%20beautiful%20lie.

4. Chubbuck, I. (2004). *The Power of the Actor.* New York: Gotham Books.

5. http://www.urbanimprov.org/.

6. See for example John O'Toole and Bruce Burton, *Acting Against Bullying: Using Drama and Peer Teaching to Reduce Bullying,* http://www.education.com/reference/article/act-against-reduce-bullying-peer-teaching/?page=3.

7. I actually think this popular quotation may be a distortion of Isadora's actual comment, "If I were only a dancer, I would not speak." See p. i, Rosemount, F. (Ed.). (1994). *Isadora Speaks: Writings and Speeches of Isadora Duncan.* Chicago: Kerr.

8. See *The Silent Epidemic,* p. v.

9. For extensive discussion of the changing voices of arts education advocacy, see my recent book, *Why Our Schools Need the Arts.* (2007). New York: Teachers College Press.

Chapter 3: Ambiguity

1. See Davis, J. (2000). Metacognition and Multiplicity: The Arts as Agents to Different Hues of Thought. In M. Shaughnessy (Ed.), *Educational Psychology Review, 12*(3), 339–359. New Haven, CT: Yale University Press.

2. Please note that my take on the readiness of high school students for identification with the artist differs from that of some aesthetic stage theorists. For discussions of these theorists (e.g., Housens), children responding to works of art in the museum, and Nelson Goodman's reflections on the construction of emotion by a non-emoting artist, see Davis, J. (2008). *Why Our Schools Need the Arts.* New York: Teachers College Press; and Davis, J. (2007). *Framing Education as Art: The Octopus Has a Good Day.* New York: Teachers College Press; and Davis, J. (1996). the MUSE (Museums Uniting with Schools in Education) Book, Cambridge, MA: President and Fellows of Harvard College.

3. Shakespeare, W. (1599). *The Tragedy of Romeo and Juliet.* New York; Signet Classic; Leonard Bernstein (music), Stephen Sondheim (lyrics), and Arthur Laurents (script), *West Side Story* (1957).

4. Hawthorne, N. (1994). *The Scarlet Letter.* New York: Norton Classic; *Easy A* (2010), written by Bert V. Royal and directed by Will Gluck.

5. *Boyz n the Hood* (1991), written and directed by John Singleton.

6. *Precious* (2009), screenplay by Geoffrey Fletcher based on the novel *Push* by Sapphire, directed by Lee Daniels.

7. See for example Russell, S. T., & Joyner, K. (2001, August). Adolescent Sexual Orientation and Suicide Risk, Evidence from a National Study. *American Journal of Public Health, 91*(8), 1276–1281.

8. See for a wonderful example www.itgetsbetter.org.

9. See Duncum, P., & Bracey, T. (Eds.). (2001). *On Knowing: Art and Visual Culture.* Christchurch, New Zealand: Canterbury University Press, p. 210.

Chapter 4: Process Orientation

1. Csikszentmihalyi, M. *Flow: The Psychology of Optimal Experience* (New York: Harper & Row, 1990).

2. See http://www.youthradio.org.

3. See an interview with Lissa Soep at http://www.hightechhigh.org/unboxed/issue2/learning_as_production/.

4. Sutherland, D. (producer/director). *Jack Levine: Feast of Pure Reason* [videotape] (Newton, MA: David Sutherland Productions, 1986).

5. Davis, J. (2005, September). Redefining Ratso Rizzo: Learning from the Arts About Process and Reflection. *Phi Delta Kappan, 87*(1), 11–18. Reprinted with permission of Phi Delta Kappa International, www.pdkintl.org. All rights reserved.

6. See Strickland's center and life story: http://mcgyouthandarts.org and his book (with Vince Rause), *Make the Impossible Possible.* (2007). New York: Doubleday.

7. Quincy Mosby, "A Drop-Out Reflects and Reforms," June 7, 2005, NPR Youth Radio Story, http://www.npr.org. All rights reserved.

Chapter 5: Connection

1. Greene, M. (2007). *Imagination and the Healing Arts,* p. 4. An essay available from the Maxine Greene Foundation for Social Imagination, the Arts and Education, http://www.maxinegreene.org/articles.php.

2. See Davis, J. H. (2010).

3. Davis, J. H. (2008). *Why Our Schools Need the Arts.* New York: Teachers College Press.

4. Barrie, J. M. 1904 stage play. *Peter Pan* (1987). New York: Henry Holt & Co.

5. See Davis (2008), pp. 14–24, for an overview of the different configurations of the arts in education.

6. Ibid., pp. 48–70, for more detailed descriptions of each of the five features and the attendant outcomes.

7. The 1996 novel (by Sapphire, NY: Vintage) on which the movie *Precious* is based.

8. See Davis (2005), pp. 106–111 for discussion of cultural continuum (wheel of Culture) perpetuated through art.

9. Dahl, R. (1961). *James and the Giant Peach.* New York: Alfred Knopf.

Chapter 6: With an Eye to the Future

1. See *The Silent Epidemic.*

2. Ravitch, D. (2011, February 13). Closing Public Schools: A Truly Bad Idea. *Education Week,* http://blogs.edweek.org/edweek/Bridging-Differences/2011/02/closing_public_schools_a_truly.html.

3. See for example The American Diploma Project, www.achieve.org/adp-network.

4. See theories from Erikson to Freud nicely summarized in pp. 546–547 of Gardner, H. (1982). *Developmental Psychology: An Introduction* (2nd ed.). Boston: Scott Foresman.

5. See Williams, M., Cross, D., Hong, J., Aultman, L., Osbon, J., & Schutz, P. (2008). There Are No Emotions in Math. *Teachers College Record, 110*(8), 1574–1610

INDEX

ABOUT THE AUTHOR

Jessica Hoffmann Davis is a writer, teacher, and researcher with an abiding interest in children and art. At Harvard's Graduate School of Education, Dr. Davis was the Bauman and Bryant Senior Lecturer, the founder and first director of the Arts in Education Program, and a principal investigator at Project Zero. Her research has primarily focused on arts learning and development within and beyond school walls, as well as the arts-related research methodology known as portraiture (see, for example, *The Art and Science of Portraiture*, co-authored with Sara Lawrence-Lightfoot). Widely published in monographs and academic journals, Davis's recent books include *Framing the Arts as Education: The Octopus Has a Good Day* (2005), *Why Our Schools Need the Arts* (2008), and *Ordinary Gifted Children: The Power and Promise of Individual Attention* (2010, all published by Teachers College Press). Her author website is www.jessicahoffmanndavis.com.